the

first

move

the first move

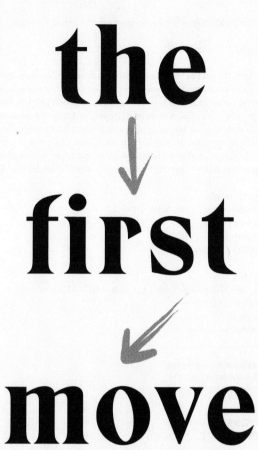

**Break the dating
rules to find a bigger
love and better life**

EMILY J. BROOKS

murdoch books
Sydney | London

Published in 2020 by Murdoch Books, an imprint of Allen & Unwin

Murdoch Books Australia
83 Alexander Street, Crows Nest NSW 2065
Phone: +61 (0)2 8425 0100
murdochbooks.com.au
info@murdochbooks.com.au

Murdoch Books UK
Ormond House, 26–27 Boswell Street, London WC1N 3JZ
Phone: +44 (0) 20 8785 5995
murdochbooks.co.uk
info@murdochbooks.co.uk

A catalogue record for this
book is available from the
National Library of Australia

ISBN 978 1 76052 549 1 Australia
ISBN 978 1 91163 268 9 UK

Cover design by Patti Andrews
Text design by Emily O'Neill
Typeset by Midland Typesetters
Printed and bound in Australia by Griffin Press

10 9 8 7 6 5 4 3 2 1

The paper in this book is FSC certified.
FSC promotes environmentally responsible,
socially beneficial and economically viable
management of the world's forests.

To my girlfriends,
who always did it for the story.

'The truth will set you free, but first it will piss you off.'

Gloria Steinem

Contents

Author's Note

This book is built on a question that involves a certain level of privilege to even ask. When I talk about the challenges successful women face in romance I am aware of the links to education and wealth and opportunity. As a white cis woman, I acknowledge not only my marginalisation but also my privilege, and I have not tackled this question because I think it is the greatest issue we face.

This book also involves an exploration of hetero-sexual relationships, and of how gendered roles created long ago for 'women' and 'men' still influence the paths we walk today. Same-sex and non-binary partnerships do not experience the same problems; in fact, some research reveals they are showing us the way. When I write about 'women', I aim to do so as inclusively as possible. Gender is not biological, but a socially enforced—and personal—identity. It impacts how we see ourselves in the world, and how the world sees us. Other factors further influencing our experiences include race, disability, religion and sexuality. This book draws on social research as well as my own life experience and the experiences of those I know. To borrow the words of Henry Thoreau, I am confined to—and can only write from—the narrowness of my experience. So, when I make generalisations, they may not be the experience of every person reading. I have not written this book to divide, but to improve our lives. Not all of it will apply to you, but I hope you take what is useful.

Preface

I have always written myself out of trouble. Only some-times do I write myself into it. I write entirely to figure out what I am thinking about the world I inhabit and my place in it. Usually I find clarity and, on a good day, meaning. So, I always suspected I would write a book. Never, though, did I think it would be about love.

If I am to be honest with you on these pages, which is what I will be, I never cared much for dating as a younger woman. I have listened to—and been the counsel-lor in—countless conversations about whom this person was dating and why and what happened, and I would always grow bored quickly knowing I would be hearing about someone else the following week. The topic seemed trivial. The act itself, a waste of time. It was fair to say, I'd been burned. I didn't trust love, so I wrote it (and the men who could offer it) off. Only a little later in life did the scar of heartbreak fade and I grew to enjoy the stories and embrace some of my own. Small acts of hope and amusement, and maybe subconsciously I knew they were material. As Nora Ephron loved to say, 'Everything is copy,' and as my girlfriends love to say, 'Do it for the story.' There was no downside. If the date was good, great. If the date was terrible, it was entertainment for the rest of us. Now, I guess, those stories make up the sum of a much bigger one. This book.

My early lack of interest in the topic at large is something I both blame and thank my parents for. My mother encouraged me to steer clear of boys as romantic pursuits in the playground while other mothers pushed their daughters into them. I was encouraged, instead, to work. My father, fortunately or unfortunately, depending on the day you speak to him, has three daughters. I am the first. So he pushed me, I would argue, like every first son. You put in the work, you did your best, and usually it paid off. 'The world is your oyster,' he would preach. So, I kept putting in the work and doing my best and, while it did not pay off in sports requiring any sort of coordination, it paid off at school. I excelled. As a result, I grew up believing I could be anything I wanted. I was limited only by my ambition.

So, I had buckets of it.

I walked this ambition right into a job with the biggest women's magazine in the country before I finished my first degree or enjoyed my twenty-first birthday. But over the next decade, my perception shifted. When people discovered I was working for one of the most powerful women in Australian media, they vomited the same double-barrelled question: 'Is she married? Does she have kids?' *Of all the questions, that is your first?* I would wonder. I don't recall ever hearing that question asked of a successful man. Neither women nor men seemed to believe that success and love could coexist for women, as it does for men.

At the same time, I was collecting girlfriends as ambitious as I was. Each year we claimed a little more success in our careers, but rarely did we find success in romance. Men would hang around for a while, only to disappear. Then I stumbled on an entire body of research that pointed to a possible reason: successful, highly educated women have, throughout history, faced a penalty in romance. Was my mother right when she said we were too intimidating? My boss, my friends, me; were we all just too intimidating?

And then there were my colleagues at the magazine, who were closer to my mother's age than mine. I listened as these women in their thirties and forties pitched stories about how limited the world still was for women—limited by unconscious bias, and gender discrimination, and sexual abuse, and domestic violence, and statistics showing that women lead just 2.8 per cent of the world's top 500 companies. This number is so dismal, we're now dodging the corporate glass ceiling to build ourselves entirely new houses—our own companies—only to receive around 3 per cent of venture-capital funding globally. (For women of colour, it is less than 1 per cent.) Then, of course, there's the paradoxical conundrum that our reproductive system begins to deteriorate around the same time we're set to excel in the workforce. And if we choose to make use of our reproductive system, it's statistically likely we'll be the ones compromising our career while bearing the brunt of unpaid work in the home. With each conversation overheard and story filed, my eyes opened. Then the fury kicked in.

It seemed I was not limited only by my ambition. The world, for women, was completely limited. My naivety evolved into bewilderment and my oyster disappeared. And ever since then, my work has been driven by hope for the freedom I thought we had, and the frustration that we don't yet have it.

I became that person at parties who, after two champagnes, began lecturing men about the gender pay gap and women about emotional labour. On the receiving end were my friends in their twenties, many of whom were yet to fully realise their limitations. We had come from safe, caring homes and were predominantly white cis women driving our young lives toward the destination of self-actualisation, steered by a lack of compromise. Privilege is invisible to those who have it, they say. It is also blinding. You don't see inequality until it punches you in the face—and most of them hadn't taken the hit yet. This was before Harvey Weinstein, #MeToo and the fourth wave of feminism really took hold. My girlfriends hadn't come up against discrimination in senior leadership roles or gendered assumptions around motherhood. They were not bosses or mothers yet, so they didn't fully consider equality when they dated. Their romantic rudder was guided by connection and personality and job title, more so than whether the guy before them would share the load of unpaid work and parenthood.

As I sat between the older women who knew our limitations and the younger women who did not, the penny dropped. If you found a partner who saw your life as equal to his in the beginning, wouldn't that soften the blow of gendered roadblocks down the track? Shouldn't we be thinking about it now before it's all too late? Why don't we discuss equality in modern romance like we debate parental leave and quotas? I guess everyone still views it as trivial, like I once did. If we want equality in our relationships, we need to think about it and talk about it *before* we walk into it. We need to realign our behaviour in the early stages of romance to better reflect the gender-equal partnerships we want—whether we realise we want them yet or not.

Before you read on, it is important that you know who I am. I am a woman who, at this point, has never considered having children, or becoming a wife. The first time I attended the wedding of one of my closest girl-friends, I wore black. I was in mourning, I said. We laughed about it because that was apparently standard behaviour from yours truly and the bride knew better than to be offended. I was thrilled for her, as I am thrilled for every girlfriend who walks down the aisle, but when it comes to my own relationship with the word 'wife', I have never been able to successfully consolidate it into my identity. I have spent the past four years with a man I would like to spend the rest of my life with, but as Jia Tolentino wrote for *The New Yorker*, 'Me? I find myself thinking. *A wife? In this economy?*'

This has freed me, in a sense, from the anxiety of the biological clock, and I have been able to treat love like the irrational, unpredictable thing it is without my age hovering over each relationship like a lingering, darkening cloud. Finding a Great Love to wander through life with has always been a desire, more than a necessity, which has made me feel like I view romance somewhat differently to many women. Some would say, I have been able to view it like a man does. Deadline free. This has provided me with a unique lens to examine and observe the problems women face in their search for love. My focus has been channelled outward, rather than inward. And as I have watched my friends being penalised for being smarter than their dates, seen single women talk themselves down in front of men, done it occasionally myself, and observed young women wander through romance blissfully unaware of the inequities to come, I have been compelled to write it all down. I hope through this book I have written a few of us out of trouble.

This book contains advice, but it is advice based less on personal opinion and more around solutions to counteract a social problem. This book also leans on social research as much as my life experience. Importantly, this book has some answers but it does not have all the answers. I hope, in fact, it prompts some questions: about the world you occupy and your place in it and, maybe most importantly, why you operate within it the way you do. Most of all, I hope this book delivers equal hope and frustration, for that is how we maintain progress and keep all women moving forward. And eventually, we will reach a time when young women move out of home and into the workforce to discover they were not living with naive thoughts at all. They are only limited by themselves.

Introduction: Leaving the Rules Behind

The women I know are liberated at work but confused in love. When it comes to our careers, we have solid visions and five-year plans, but in romance we don't know how to ask for what we want, let alone demand it. Most of us dance around our desires, conforming our identities and twisting our needs to better suit the guy we are dating. We might be free to make the first move, but we are also warned by dating books, girlfriends and mothers that our active initiation is still a problem. We are told to lean in at work but wait for him to call. To ask for the pay rise but not his number. We send confident emails to clients all day, but at night our texts are approved by three girlfriends before they're sent to that guy we met last week. While women have grown into self-actualised humans with our own careers and lives and Bumble accounts, we're still unsure whether men truly accept—let alone desire—the women we have become.

There is good reason for this.

Throughout modern history the successful professional woman has been unsuccessful in love. My girlfriend calls them the Successfully Unsuccessful. Most of the women I know have been (or still are) Successfully Unsuccessful.

The promotions come every two years but the good men never seem to arrive—let alone call them back. This confusion has become an invisible anxiety many young women feel but cannot quite articulate, and it has been left unanswered for so long because of where we have channelled our focus.

We are all by now familiar with the discourse around gender inequality, which has remained largely focused on work and the family home. Workplaces and board meetings are dominated by talk of unconscious bias, quotas versus targets and the reality that—according to the 2017 World Economic Forum—the global gender pay gap won't be eliminated for another 217 years. The once private matters of the home are now in the public domain as parental-leave schemes are highlighted, childcare subsidies are debated and stay-at-home fathers receive a round of applause from the entire western world. All this, despite the reality that women still bear the brunt of unpaid work in the home and, if they have children, are more likely to work part-time or not at all.

As we have guided the public discussion toward these two spheres of our lives, we have forgotten where 'the juggle' between work and home begins. It begins, of course, with love. Modern romance and dating have been largely ignored, even though this is where the power dynamic for a couple is set. If we get it right here, surely the rest of our lives will be made easier. And if we get it wrong, how can we expect an equal relationship at all?

In 1995, millions of liberated single women purchased and followed a book called *The Rules,* which told them that women's newfound independence was the problem preventing them from finding a husband. The answer lay in hiding their success, in reshaping their independence into indifference. Men like to hunt. You must allow yourself to be hunted. Men need a project. You must be the project. It was, essentially, the traditional game of playing 'hard to get': if you appear not to need love, you will probably find it. A performance of distance, to ensure companionship. What, one might ask, were these women going to do once they found a husband? Finally become themselves and demand the love they desired, expecting their husbands to change and to happily provide emotional support, help with the dishes, and pick the kids up from school on Tuesday, please? *The Rules* was so focused on helping women lock down a husband, it ignored what these newly independent women actually wanted from men: more.

Women have evolved since the mid-nineties, and so have men, but the rhetoric—the stories we tell each other and ourselves—has yet to catch up. Women know what we want: an equal relationship. We want the man we love and respect to love us and respect our career as much as his. If we have children, we want to share the load.

We don't want to stand behind our future husbands, we want to stand alongside them. If compromise and sacrifice are required, we want it to be equal compromise and sacrifice, made together with a shared goal.

We want these equal relationships, but we're unsure how to demand them. As a result, our dating scripts do not yet reflect the gender-equal partnerships we desire. We do not play by *The Rules* anymore, but the residue remains. We fumble our way through romance, telling ourselves we're empowered to do whatever we want but not fully believing our internal monologue. We ignore our intuition, overthink and view ourselves through the male gaze instead of our own. We may send nudes and demand casual sex, but is that just fulfilling a male desire built on rigorous porn consumption? Are we demanding the love we desire with the same vigour? We still wander into first dates thinking *I hope he likes me* instead of *I hope I like him*, and we still talk ourselves down in front of men out of fear we will be penalised. If we truly claim our lives and desires, we wonder, will it compromise our ability to find love entirely? If we own our independence and ambition, will we end up Successfully Unsuccessful? Can success and love coexist for women, like it does for men?

Fortunately, throughout the process of writing this book, I have discovered that this shift is well on its way to happening. The successful, educated woman does not have to follow the same rules her mother did, as the picture of today reveals a slightly more positive story. Young men's perceptions have shifted, albeit slowly, and the penalty the successful, educated woman so often faced in romance is one we are hitting less and less often. Things are changing, but we still, unfortunately, come up against it. If we don't give progress a nudge, we will be coaching our daughters through this very same issue; and if we don't rewrite this story, the successful woman will continue to believe the outdated one.

The stories we have been told throughout history feed the invisible anxiety that still has a tight hold of the modern woman, keeping her permanently unsure of herself in love. The outdated narrative that we are powerless without manipulation in romance continues to hand the power to men, and the narrative that success is our greatest problem encourages us to further shrink ourselves. How can we expect an equal love and a fulfilling relationship if we won't state *who we are* and *what we want*?

The Rules encouraged women to play an old game, but what if we owned our independence and ambition and success instead of trying to hide them? If this is our only route to finding an equal love, we must take it. We must claim the power within ourselves if we are to demand more. There is little to lose, and so much to gain.

Through this book I want to help you realign your approach in romance to find a more equal love, a love that allows you to reach your full potential as your partner reaches his. For we now know that equal relationships are more satisfying than the alternative. We also know that the long-term relationship you choose is one of the most important decisions of your life. When I spoke to Rae Cooper, Associate Dean at the University of Sydney Business School and Professor of Gender, Work and Employment Relations, she said, 'Picking the right partner is as important as picking the right degree for you, or picking the right employer. Of course you have to have affection and love in there as well to make you happy, but having someone who supports you in your career and what you want to do for the rest of your life, I think, exerts more of an impact on your success than who you work for.'

Our personal and professional lives are inextricably linked, and to ignore one is to enter a fight with one hand tied behind our back. When we address it, our growth is exponential. This book is about women's progress as much as it is about modern love. When women find the love we deserve, it lifts up the rest of our lives. So, we must fight for it. We must demand it. That fight, I guess, is where this book starts.

Chapter 1

The Notorious RBG and R-E-S-P-E-C-T

There is a saying, that behind every great man is a woman rolling her eyes. And another, that behind every great woman is a 'Marty'. Jim Carrey told the world the first and I made up the latter. But there is good reason behind my made-up saying. Let me explain.

The year was 1951, the destination was Cornell University in Ithaca, New York, and the woman was tiny. She was just five feet tall, seventeen years old and had been sent to Cornell because it was the preferred university for parents to send their daughters. Not because the grounds were safe, or the classes well regarded. Because there were four men to every woman there. So, if you couldn't find a husband at Cornell you were, well, screwed. This tiny woman didn't have big problems at Cornell. During her first year, she didn't need to repeat a class or agree to a second date. She kept her options wide open. Until she found herself on a date with a very tall man. Marty.

Marty was the life of the party while she preferred to quietly watch it. And what she noticed throughout her

time quietly watching parties at Cornell was that the brilliant women tended to suppress their smarts in front of
the men. And the men either didn't notice or simply played
along with the time-honoured tradition. But not Marty.
He was different. He was the first man to like her *more*
for her mind. In fact, he was the first man to pay any
attention to her mind at all. So, this tiny woman went on
a second date. And a third. And eventually, she graduated
with both a degree and a husband.

Marty was one year ahead of her, so she followed him
to Harvard Law. She was one of only nine women in her
Harvard Law class of more than 500 students. At the
beginning of her first year in 1954 she attended the Dean's
dinner held for only the women, during which the Dean
asked each guest why she was taking a seat that could
be occupied by a man. Over the following years, this tiny
woman proved her seat's worth. By her second year she
became the first woman to make the Law Review.

But behind the shine of milestones was the work ethic
of a woman doing it all with a two-year-old child and a
sick husband. In her second year, Marty was diagnosed
with testicular cancer. While he underwent treatment,
she did her work and his, averaging two hours' sleep each
night. It was a time that tested not only her strength but
established just how far she could push herself. Eventually
Marty recovered, graduated and was snapped up by a firm

in New York City, moving the family of three to the Big Apple. This tiny woman finished her final year at Columbia University while sitting on the Law Review, tied as first in her class, and went out into the big, wide world, only to realise she was a woman. And no firm in New York City would hire her.

She was the only woman to ever sit on two Law Reviews and she couldn't get a job.

While watching her husband become New York City's top tax lawyer, this tiny woman took her many firsts and found her feet in academia, becoming a professor at Rutgers Law School in 1963. She covered mainly civil procedure until some of her students convinced her to take a class on gender law. She didn't know it at the time, but it was the beginning of something special. The class, called 'Women and the Law', was reflective of the times in the United States, where the second wave of feminism was creating tidal waves of change. Women all over the country, and the western world, were waking up to realise they were second-class citizens, demanding reproductive rights and equality in the workplace, fighting sexual discrimination and domestic violence, and asking for the right to apply for their own mortgages and credit cards. They filled the streets, they protested, they wrote books speaking to a sector of society that had never properly been spoken to, they created women's circles, they built magazines, and the consciousness-raising began. They could finally be heard, so they raised their voices and then some.

But this tiny woman's soft voice and quiet tempera-ment didn't lend her to protesting in the streets. So, she took her bright mind and big thoughts, and plowed them into what she knew—the law. She co-founded the Women's Rights Project at the American Civil Liberties Union and took on cases where women (and men) were discrimi-nated against on the basis of gender. Her genius lay in her counterintuitive approach. She strategically took on cases where subversive laws appeared to benefit women but in fact increased their dependency on men. And with each case, she weaved a web quietly changing the legal land-scape to help women exist in the workplace without being legally discriminated against on the basis of their gender. From 1973 to 1976, she argued six gender-discrimination cases in the US Supreme Court and won five.

This tiny woman with a big mission was Ruth Bader Ginsburg.

And whether American women knew it or not, their lives were being changed by the consistent work of her mind and drive, which eventually led her to the other side of the bench on the US Supreme Court. Ruth Bader Ginsburg is the second woman in history to become a US Supreme Court Justice, and at her confirmation hearing back in 1993, she said she would not be sitting in this particular chair, in this particular room, without the determined efforts of women and men who aspired for equality. But there was one man in particular. 'I have had the great good fortune to share life with a partner truly extraordinary for his generation. A man who believed at age eighteen, when we met, that a woman's work, whether at home or on the job, is as important as a man's,' Bader Ginsburg said. 'I became a lawyer in days when women were not wanted by most members of the legal profession. I became a lawyer because Marty supported that choice unreservedly.'

When you insert Marty back into the story of Ruth Bader Ginsburg, you see a man who saw value in a woman for her mind. A man who respected that mind so much he encouraged it into the law. A man who took the front seat for the first part of their lives, but the back seat when the time called for it. A man who raised their two children, while his wife worked late into the night, calling her to come home for dinner and again, much later, when it was time to go to bed. And a man whose wife would not be a US Supreme Court Justice without him. See, Ruth Bader Ginsburg openly admits she would not have secured the job without her husband. Not because she wasn't worthy. Not because she was a woman. Because she wasn't loud, but Marty was, and—as a result—he was also well connected. He campaigned day in and day out for his wife. As US Court of Appeals Judge Harry T. Edwards said in the 2018 documentary *RBG*, 'He was so in love with his wife and so respected her as a real giant in the legal profession, he felt it would be an outrage if she wasn't seriously considered.' Marty got Ruth the interview. But she got the job. Within fifteen minutes of meeting her, President Bill Clinton was sold. And since then, the entire world has grown to love The Notorious RBG and bear witness to a partnership that was truly extraordinary for its generation.

Turning the Extraordinary into Ordinary

It's not often a confirmation hearing brings you to tears, but a YouTube video of Ruth Bader Ginsburg's confirmation to the US Supreme Court—filmed nearly three decades ago—made me cry. It wasn't her speech that did it, and they weren't the type of tears some would consider 'cute'. They were not cute. There was no single tear sparkling on a cheekbone as I sat upright, hair in place, composure intact. They were the type that put you sideways on the couch. But the kicker wasn't, *'I have had the great good fortune to share life with a partner truly extraordinary for his generation . . .'* It was Marty's face. As Ruth spoke, behind her shoulder sat Marty, head down, glasses on, grin intact, as he appeared to mentally transport himself back to the moment he met this extraordinary woman. You could see their first date play out in the twinkle of his eye. The private slideshow wasn't downloadable, but it was obvious his love for her went beyond love, and moved into a less conventional territory. See, men have loved their wives for lifetimes. This was something different. Something acute. It was professional respect. And in the public arena, this evolves into something else. It grows wings and takes form as quiet pride.

There's nothing exceptional about a wife sitting behind her husband with professional respect, quiet pride. We have seen it on our televisions for decades. The First Lady holding the bible as her husband takes the oath swearing him in as the next President or Prime Minister. She claps with the crowd, wearing that knowing smile. It's the smile of a teammate who stepped aside, however briefly, to make the coffee or hold the hand, to ease the pain of the tough nights fought through to get here. To this moment. Where the rest of the world, or room, coalesces to witness and acknowledge the brilliance of this person. Her person. And she sits there, in the crowd, wearing that knowing smile. We know that story. We've seen that story.

But to see a husband sit behind his wife as she is nominated for one of the most honourable seats in the United States, wearing that knowing smile, is something less traditional. It is something that crosses gender lines. It is extraordinary. And it reminded me of something Lindy West wrote for *The New York Times* after Hillary Clinton lost the 2016 US Presidential election. I had saved that article and revisited it over the years. In the article, West wrote about seeing Bill Clinton beam as his wife cast her vote on election day. 'We're accustomed to that pride flowing the other direction, from wife to husband . . .' she wrote. 'It is normal for men to have ambition. It is normal for women to stand aside.' Now, a similar beam made me cry like a possessed woman in a small apartment watching a YouTube clip on a Friday night while the rest of the world was out drinking martinis. And that is why we are here, on page 14, of a book about finding a more equal love.

Because as women have fought through four waves of feminism—to secure the vote, to be able to work and be rewarded for this work equally, to own our own bank accounts and homes and bodies and lives, to step into the world closer to first-class citizens than second—we have grown into evolved humans with hopes and dreams equal to men's. We are not there yet, but our ambitions are. And as we step forward in all facets of life—including sometimes public life—many of us would like a teammate to stand beside us, and sometimes behind us. Throughout history, it has been normal for women to step aside. Yet as we leap forward in our own lives, it is not yet normal for men to do the same. It is still extraordinary to find a Marty, when it should be ordinary.

A New Kind of Love

There is a name for this extraordinary love, and in order to make it ordinary, I must first tell you about it. It is Teammate Love. And this love, while still only stumbled upon by a fortunate few, is the love starting to lift women up in this world.

Teammate Love is an energy existing between a couple that can be recognised in a look.* It isn't showy. It doesn't perform. It is usually witnessed in a quick glance, a knowing nod. Or it is found, in longer periods, when one teammate listens to the other, who usually has a captive audience. They pay attention to the other with professional as well as personal respect. Collectively, it is a look worn by a couple that makes you wonder, *Where can I find that?* This look makes you question your romantic choices, unless you have Teammate Love, in which case you don't

* DISCLAIMER: Teammate Love is not dissimilar to Big Dick Energy, or BDE. If you don't remember BDE, it was all the internet talked about for one great week in June 2018 and was best defined by Allison P. Davis in an article she wrote for The Cut about Pete Davidson—which you definitely do remember.

bat an eyelid. It is the superior love of all the loves because the partners are peers. They are, above all else, a team, and this requires passing the ball between them. Most importantly, they respect what their teammate does when they have the ball.

Teammate Love is most easily evidenced by the couples who have it. It is the Prince Harry and Meghan Markle kind of love. Not Prince William and Kate. It is the Michelle and Barack Obama kind of love. It is the Bill and Melinda Gates kind of love. It is the John Legend and Chrissy Teigen kind of love. The Kanye West and Kanye West kind of love. The RBG and Marty kind of love.

Behind this love is a partnership that is on the side of progress. It is not a partnership based on the traditional gender roles of homemaker and breadwinner and an exchange of these services. It is a partnership based on *real conversation* and *real negotiation*. Historically in relationships, men's ambitions and lives have taken priority over women's, but Teammate Love understands that the two people in it are equal partners with equal lives, and one teammate's priorities do not automatically trump the other's. Every decision is made together—it means more compromise for men, and more agency for women, yes, but this compromise is a fair one that allows both teammates to live full, more satisfied lives. It does not push men down to pull women up, it simply evens the keel, which leaves everyone happier. As a result, there is more connection, less resentment, and maybe most importantly, more empathy for each other's path—because you are usually walking a similar one. This is a love I hope soon becomes ordinary. But before we look at how to find Teammate Love, it is important, I guess, to examine how we arrived here.

The Four Stages of Love

Today's woman wants a teammate over a knight, and with good reason. We live in a world filled with a different kind of desire, because, well, the trials and tribulations of our time are different to those of the women who have come before us. We have changed, and so has our perception of what makes a viable partner in this life. Because in its early days, love had nothing to do with marriage. While we deal with the technical conundrum of unwanted men sliding into our DMs, women, for thousands of years, faced the far greater challenge of marrying a man they didn't love.

Before Love

Before the late eighteenth century, women and men did not marry for love or even something as trivial as lust. It was purely a political and economic move orchestrated by families. 'Marriage was invented to get in-laws,' explained Stephanie Coontz, author, historian and

Director of Research and Public Education for the Council on Contemporary Families in the United States, to whom I spoke extensively about this issue. 'It was a way of turning strangers into relatives, of making peace.' The word wife actually means 'peaceweaver' in many languages, as marriage was a way of improving the sociopolitical position of families. 'As such it became a centre for maneuvering and control and coercion and betrayal for thousands and thousands of years.' The upper class used it to form military alliances or consolidate wealth or climb a little higher on the ladder of social power. The middle classes used it to do good business. And even the lower classes benefitted from it, growing their family labor force and forming more connections. Everyone was happy! Except, maybe, the two people in the marriage. But that didn't matter. For thousands of years, it wasn't about them; it was for the greater good of everyone else. Marriage was, Coontz said, 'much too important to leave it up to individual choice, and especially an individual choice based on something so irrational as the feeling of love'.

Good Enough Love

When the late eighteenth century rolled around, something shifted. The Enlightenment, also known as The Age Of Reason, was a philosophical movement that caused the young (primarily in Europe and, later, in North America) to question the world order. They didn't want to be told what to do, or think, by the older generations or the state. So, they started to write their own rules. Around this time, American and French revolutions also occurred. The Declaration of Independence was written in the United States, which pronounced that people (meaning white land-owning men) were entitled to their own pursuit of happiness, and that extended to their personal relationships. So, women and men tried to pursue marriage through the lens of love. According to Coontz, this scared conservatives, who feared that if men loved their wives, they might start listening to them and everything would fall apart. The scarier concern, though, was that people would demand the right to divorce if love ended. 'In other words,' said Coontz, 'they were frightened that love might be the death of marriage.'

So for the next 150 years, all the way up until the 1950s and 1960s, people started marrying for love, but those perceived 'destabilising aspects'—that conservatives feared would destroy society—were kept in line by laws in western countries. Divorce was restricted and dictated by the state, and having a 'love child' out of wedlock was greeted with condemnation by the community. But the biggest barrier to a partnership built upon love were the strict gender roles husbands and wives were legally confined to. It wasn't just a matter of societal expectations—it was a matter of survival.

Women couldn't own their own home, open their own bank account or—in most cases—work beyond the roles of typist, nurse or teacher. Most lived with their parents until they found a husband. So, in order to do basic adult things, have basic adult freedoms and survive, a woman needed a man who could hold down a job and provide her with income and security. Meanwhile, a man needed a woman who could pop out a couple of children, keep his home in decent check and whip up a mean lasagne. Consequently, while love had come into the equation, the masses still had to choose their husband or wife on the basis of their ability to fulfil these roles. Let's call this 'Good Enough' love. Even as late as 1967, in a study of 1,079 American college students, 76 per cent of the women claimed they would be willing to marry someone they didn't love, while only 35 per cent of the men said the same. The men, you see, had less riding on it. They could live a basic adult life without a wife, so they had more time and, as a result, more options.

And then Betty Friedan and *The Feminine Mystique* came along.

Soulmate Love

When the second wave of feminism arrived in the 1960s, women woke up to realise they were spending their lives being sold cleaning products, because their only role in society was to manage their home and raise their children. And they weren't happy about it. Women took to the streets across the western world, demanding the right to exist outside the home and climb the professional ladder without limits. After more than a decade of protesting, forming political alliances and demanding to be heard in the corridors of power, women of this era won major victories, such as the 1963 Equal Pay Act in the United States. In Australia, before winning equal pay for equal work in 1969, women won the right to be both a wife and a worker when in October 1966 the Holt government finally repealed the Marriage Bar—the government stipulation that any woman who married was 'deemed to have retired from the Commonwealth service upon her marriage'; essentially ending her career—that had plagued Australian women's lives since Federation.

As women gained rights and flooded into workplaces, Good Enough Love wasn't really good enough anymore. A woman didn't need a husband to bring home the bacon if she could bring it home herself. From the late 1960s, women no longer wanted a reliable bank in a husband—they wanted a soulmate, someone they could truly connect with. By the 1990s, 91 per cent of American women said they would not marry someone without the presence of romantic love.

Psychologist Abraham Maslow's classic hierarchy of needs explains, in part, why this occurred. The three levels to Maslow's hierarchy form a pyramid, illustrating basic human needs in level of priority: *basic needs* on the bottom, followed by *psychological needs* and finally *self-fulfillment* needs. Thanks to the second wave of feminism, women could achieve basic needs (such as food and shelter) by themselves. And once they had sorted these out, they looked up the pyramid to *psychological needs*, which include esteem (a feeling of accomplishment, hence the whole fighting-for-the-right-to-work thing) but also belongingness and love, which includes both friendships and intimate relationships. Women could achieve some *psychological needs* through friendships, but romantic love—that was something a husband could help with. So, they went in search of a soulmate instead of a man with the appropriate job title (although some still did, and still do, the latter), and it shifted the institution of marriage.

By 1990 in the United States, the median marriage age for women jumped up to twenty-four, after sitting between twenty and twenty-two for more than a century. Economic independence allowed women to wait for the right love and to delay marriage and children. By 1995, *The New York Times* stated, 'Women are becoming equal providers', citing US Bureau of Labor Statistics data that reported that married women who worked full time throughout 1993 contributed on average 41 per cent of the family's income.

It appeared women could, in fact, have it all, but there was one small problem: women were now doing two jobs. They were doing the majority of parenting while also working. For society has not encouraged men to embrace fatherhood as enthusiastically as women have embraced full-time employment (for example, in 1991, only 4 per cent of Australian men with children under eighteen were stay-at-home fathers). Soulmate Love has left women with career fulfillment, a great love, and the opportunity to procreate, but also compromised and exhausted. The young women growing up today see their future ahead and, as a result, not all of us are sure we want to subscribe. Instead we are trying to change the game through the love we desire.

Teammate Love

Today, women now outnumber men at universities around the western world. This rise in education speaks directly to our career ambition, which has flowed into the love we desire. We have seen what our mothers went through, and we are learning the lessons from their lives. We want the career fulfillment, the great love and the opportunity to procreate, but we don't want to be left compromised and exhausted with two jobs. We also want self-actualisation, which we've seen is fairly difficult to achieve when you have two jobs. Running a corporation and a household is no longer the dream, because we have seen how this pans out in reality. We understand that we can't have it all at once, and therefore we must have help along the way. This means we don't just want the love of a partner who *doesn't mind* us having a career as long as we still take care of the kids and the dishes. We want a partner who has professional respect for us and will *support* our career pursuits, with an understanding that he may have to give a little. We want a Marty who will take the front seat when he needs to, but the back seat when the time calls for it; to allow us to leap forward in our own lives. And we want these moments to be decided upon through real negotiation, not gendered assumption.

However, what we want and what we currently have are two very different things. While the relationships we aspire to are now proven to be happier, more satisfied ones, they are not yet conventional or ordinary. We are on our way, but we are not there yet. The place we sit today is most accurately illustrated by a 2014 study of Harvard Business School alumni, which surveyed women and men in their thirties to their sixties. When asked about their careers and futures, less than a quarter of women in the group expected their spouse's career to take priority over theirs, but as these women's lives moved forward, their spouse's career took priority 40 per cent of the time. Meanwhile, more than half of the men in the group expected their career to take priority over that of their spouse, and this played out about three-quarters of the time. While the women of today may be able to see themselves as prime ministers or presidents or founders or bosses—with supportive partners cheering them on from the sidelines—our realities are still dragging behind. While we don't expect our partner's career to take priority over ours, it is still statistically likely his will. Wanting Teammate Love is not enough. We are sitting in a place where we must demand it, because the statistics are not yet stacking in our favour and, along the way, we are being penalised for it.

Today, the gender pay gap sits at around 14 per cent in Australia, and women are likely to retire with half the superannuation of men. The pay gap widens to more than 17 per cent in our mid-thirties to mid-forties. Gendered expectations may have evolved thanks to half a century of modern feminism, but the breadcrumbs of what was accepted fifty years ago still influence the paths we walk today. Men are still rewarded for the stability of marriage, earning on average about 15 per cent more after they marry, while women are not. It is also not a coincidence that the pay gap increases sharply for women in their mid-thirties, around the time they are told by society and their reproductive system that they should hurry along and produce a baby. As Annabel Crabb wrote in *The Wife*

Drought, 'Men's jobs are disrupted by recessions; women's jobs are disrupted by family.'

The role of 'wife' is still as a supportive figure and an economic asset to her husband, as wives bear the brunt of unpaid work (about 75 per cent globally) and childcare, while men forge on with their careers and are seen as 'responsible' providers, which is of course more achievable because they have, most likely, been relieved from the 'juggle' that women endure. In Australia, the percentage of stay-at-home fathers with children aged under eighteen has increased from 4 per cent in 1991 to around 5 per cent. I was born in 1991. The number of stay-at-home fathers has increased by 1 per cent in my lifetime.

This glacial pace of change means that the likelihood of young women dodging these figures by the time they decide to reproduce is, unfortunately, low. And the likelihood they will enjoy this juggle is also, unfortunately, low. Men's lives still often get better after marriage, while women's lives still often get worse. Married women report worse mental health and live shorter lives than single women, while married men live longer and report better mental health than single men.

I do not share all of this to depress you, but because it is crucial we understand the history we have inherited and how it shapes our future. Our choice in life partner may no longer result in us losing our job, but there are still huge impacts. It will be one of the most significant decisions we make, shifting the course of our personal and professional lives, for better or worse. If we want our success to be better than the aforementioned statistics, the odds are unfortunately stacked against us. So, we need to arrive with the best hand possible: a teammate.

When we look back throughout history, as women have climbed up Maslow's pyramid, the role of the man in our life and the love we seek has always directly spoken to the level we can reach. Good Enough Love helped us achieve *basic needs*; Soulmate Love helped us achieve *psychological needs*. Teammate Love will help us achieve *self-fulfillment needs*—which includes 'self-actualisation'—the highest point in Maslow's hierarchy of needs.

Teammate Love does not mean having a stay-at-home husband to take over every inch of unpaid work; it means passing the ball of opportunity back and forth. It means allowing women to reach their full potential, a virtue men still predominantly enjoy. Women no longer want to live in a love with gendered assumptions, or be the only one in the relationship with two jobs. We want a love that respects and encourages our pursuits, over a love that drags them down or dismisses them. I believe that women are ready for this love, and it is time we turn that grasp into a tight hold. As we have evolved to a place where women are fed up with the statistics and prepared for a better future than our mothers and grandmothers experienced, we do not search for a love that will hold us back, but a love to back us.

Chapter 2

Removing the Roadblocks

The modern professional woman has many faces and different desires but her expectations are largely the same. She expects that she can be whoever she wants to be. Beyoncé is her General, Jacinda Ardern her ally. Girls run the world, she is told. So she does. Yet as she runs her world she does so knowing that she will probably work twice as hard as the men beside her for half the remuneration. For this soundtrack of empowerment only exists because she is not yet fully empowered.

This disempowerment rears its ugly head in romance, because when the modern woman steps up to demand a new kind of love—a love less gendered and more equal—she often comes up against the roadblock so many women before her have faced: the dateability penalty. The very trait that makes the modern professional woman who she is—ambition—is the trait she is often penalised for in romance. For all the statement T-shirts and motivational memes and children's books and catchy songs, women are still held back by the invisible seatbelt of societal and cultural norms that do not yet view women's ambition as a wholly attractive trait.

She may have many desires, but she is not yet completely desirable. As Zadie Smith wrote in her collection of essays *Feel Free*, 'Things have changed, but history is not erased by change.' Modern women may operate within a narrative of limitless possibility echoed in an attempt to put the flag in gender-equal ground—despite the harsh reality that there is still so far to go—but the expectations of the past, of what is good and bad, right and wrong, slow their progress. We are still limited by history. While many of us have outgrown the idea of the traditional breadwinner and homemaker roles, their institutionalised existence is yet to be removed from society, holding us back from getting what we want. Our ambition cannot always dodge the dateability penalty. In fact, it does the opposite. It says, 'Hello, here I am. Run at me.'

The Dateability Penalty, and a Romantic Shift

The dateability penalty is recognised in different words and different stories, but it is a relatively simple concept: many men will avoid dating a woman if her success or status (ambition, education, income) exceeds his. Women, on the other hand, are overwhelmingly attracted to successful men, and the successful professional man has never had to question whether his power could handicap him on dates. In fact, research shows that a woman considers a man's intelligence, success and pay packet more important than his appearance or other factors, while the successful woman takes her ambition and excels in the labour market, only to wake up one day and question whether this success is holding her back in romance.

The dateability penalty plants itself in men's—and some women's—minds not just through societal and cultural norms of the past, but through our upbringing. As feminist writer and activist Gloria Steinem said in a 2019 *Good Weekend* interview, 'As long as children are mostly raised by women, we associate female authority with childhood. Many men, or some men, feel regressed to childhood when they see a powerful woman.'

In 2006, men surveyed in a study from Harvard and the Massachusetts Institute of Technology revealed they did not value women's intelligence or ambition when it exceeded their own. In 2007, men involved in a British study from the University of Sussex consistently preferred women with a lower socioeconomic status when considering a long-term relationship, and they perceived women with a higher education level as 'less likeable' and 'less faithful'. And in 2013 research conducted by psychologists Kate A. Ratliff of the University of Florida and

Shigehiro Oishi of the University of Virginia, men in the Netherlands and U.S. registered lower self-esteem when confronted with their romantic partner's success, while the same didn't hold true for women. However, 2015 research conducted by psychologists Marcel Zentner of the University of Innsbruck and Alice H. Eagly of Northwestern University revealed men's partner preferences are beginning to shift with increasing gender equality, but progress is slow and there are still persistent hangovers. 'It's absolutely true that there are some men still, who are quite threatened by women's achievements,' said Stephanie Coontz, 'and then there's a whole group of men who don't know they are threatened but are just a little uneasy.'

Fortunately, the dateability penalty is no longer a black-and-white issue. We are beginning to see a slow decline in this aversion to women's rising status, particularly once women are in steady relationships. Ever since women began to outnumber men in universities in the 1980s, the tendency for men to marry women with more education than themselves has steadily increased in most western countries. And in nations where the gender gap in education has reversed, it is now *more* common for a woman to have more education than her husband.

Educated women are also now more likely to marry than women without a university degree—and are less likely to divorce, which wasn't always the case. Through

the 1980s, couples in which the wife had a higher education than her husband were more likely to divorce than
those in which the wife had equal or less education. Starting in the early 1990s, however, couples who married no
longer showed added divorce risk when the wife was better
educated. 'It doesn't necessarily mean that the majority of
men have changed but enough of them have changed,' said
Coontz, 'and that's the good news.'

Yet even taking these positive shifts into account, the
research reveals a simple story: things are changing, but
not fast enough. While there are growing numbers of
women out-earning their husbands, and it is no longer
the great divorce risk, it has not increased at the rate our
higher education has. The tendency for women to marry
men with higher incomes has persisted, and it is more
common for women *with* a higher education. As we tend to
base social status on income, a man's dominant status may
not be as threatened if his wife is more educated but he still
earns more than her. If she does, he is not always happy.

In 2019, research out of the University of Bath revealed
that the men surveyed were happiest when their partners contributed to the household income—as long as it
was less than 40 per cent. When wives earned more than
40 per cent of the household income, the men reported
more psychological distress. (The outlier in this group
were men who had knowingly partnered with women

earning more than them. These men were perfectly happy for their partners to continue earning more, which shows things are moving in the right direction, albeit slowly.)

And when traditional gender roles are thrown off keel on the balance sheet, we seem to do what we can to rebalance them elsewhere. Multiple studies have shown that when wives out-earn their husbands they do more unpaid work around the house and defer to their husbands in terms of making big decisions; and in some cases, wives with a higher earning potential avoid out-earning their husbands by working part-time.

Different studies are producing different outcomes, particularly in the early stages of romance, which are always more difficult for research to monitor, but the general picture points to what I call a romantic shift. The dateability penalty is slowly shrinking—our higher education or higher earning status does not have to be the great problem it once was in marriage and relationships— and the door is open to speed up the pace of progress in our dating lives. Stephanie Coontz summarised the current scenario in one swift comment: 'There are men out there who enthusiastically embrace Teammate Love. But there are fewer of them than there are of women.' And this, my friend, is our challenge.

This romantic tension that exists as an undercurrent in women's and men's lives has been explored by Kathleen

Gerson, a Professor of Sociology and Collegiate Professor of Arts and Science at New York University, whose work focuses on the ongoing revolutions in gender, work and family life. Between 1998 and 2003, Gerson conducted 120 in-depth interviews asking young men and women who were 'children of the gender revolution' what type of relationship they hoped to have. The results show that both women and men share largely similar hopes. Most of those interviewed wanted an equal partnership—what we now call Teammate Love. However—and this is the crucial point here—when these young women and men were asked, 'Well, if you can't have that, what do you want?' most men reverted to a modified male breadwinner model and most women said, 'I want an equal relationship or I'll go it alone.' Their fallback strategies, their Plan Bs, didn't align. In fact, as Gerson wrote in her article 'What Do Women and Men Want?' published in *The American Prospect*, 'These second-best strategies are not only different but also at odds with each other.' If an egalitarian partnership were not possible, she wrote, men would choose to fall back into an arrangement allowing them to put their work first and have their partner as the primary caregiver, whereas women preferred individual autonomy over growing dependence on a husband in a traditional marriage.

This sums up the reality we now live in. Women want Teammate Love, while men have one foot in and one foot out. So, how do we finally rid ourselves of this roadblock—this persistent dateability penalty—to clear our path once and for all? It begins, of course, with removing the age-old habit of 'shrinking ourselves'. You see, while we have an opportunity to speed up progress, we're still currently downplaying our smarts to fulfil the desires of the man threatened by our success. And this needs to stop.

The Phenomenon of Shrinking Ourselves

Remember the women RBG quietly watched at Cornell parties? The women talking their 'smarts' down in front of men? Well, they were not doing this for their health. Actually, they kind of were. They were well aware of the dateability penalty and, back then, it was not a penalty they could afford to take in their stride. They had lives to fund, and that meant finding a husband, because their lives came with limits. They were completely restricted by the times. So, if a woman's success, ambition and education level exceeded that of the man in front of her, she would talk hers down in order to appear a valuable candidate for marriage. And just like those women RBG quietly watched in 1951, the modern professional woman of today with her limitless attitude still ever so quietly, ever so subtly, ever so subconsciously, talks herself down. Whether it is a learned habit from her upbringing, or the shows she watched, or the dating lessons she was taught, or the collective responses she has received after a decade of dating, at some point, she does it. She talks herself down to build up the man in front of her, or maybe just to appear less intimidating and more palatable.

When I spoke about this issue with my friend, the writer and model Jessica Vander Leahy, she told me she continues to be advised by men and women that her dual intelligence and attractiveness is far too 'intimidating' in romance. This word, *intimidating*, is one she finds deeply offensive.

> When I have heard this word said in this way I am at a loss of how to respond, because I don't think men ever get told they're intimidating because they're beautiful and smart. I think they only get told they're intimidating if they look like they're going to punch you in the face. So, it makes me think, is there something about women being smart that makes you feel equally threatened? That immediately positions me as the predator in the situation . . . It makes me feel like I have to come across as warmer and less scary.

And that, I guess, summarises the underlying frustration and bewilderment women feel when faced with the reality that our success is an apparent hindrance in romance. We are just trying to claim a little piece of this earth for ourselves, and some professional fulfillment, and enough super to retire on, and, I don't know, maybe just the independence to run our own lives however we want. Then we're told that this is somehow still offensive to part of the human race, and it infuriates us. But nevertheless, we shrink ourselves to accommodate the male ego because this is what we've been socialised to do, and we compromise ourselves in the process.

In 2017, economists Amanda Pallais of Harvard University, Thomas Fujiwara of Princeton University and Leonardo Bursztyn of the University of Chicago co-authored research called '"Acting Wife": Marriage Market Incentives and Labor Market Investments', which studied a group of MBA students and showed that young, single women downplayed their career ambitions and accomplishments in front of their classmates. These women reported lower desired salaries and less willingness to work long hours and travel for work when they thought their peers were able to see their answers versus when they were told their answers would be kept private. The answers of women in relationships, on the other hand, indicated no such change. A second study in the research showed that the problem for single women in the group was heightened when *single men* were present. These single women were 'acting wife' in order to become one.

The narrative is even reflected on relatively new television shows. In *Younger*, Kelsey Peters (played by Hilary Duff), who runs a millennial book imprint, is trying to find some 'no strings attached' romance for the night. With the help of her girlfriend, Kelsey redownloads a dating app she'd used. She starts to set up her profile again, only to realise her profile had been up the entire time and, yet, had no 'bites'. Her friend takes her phone and scours the screen for the problem:

'Oh, Kelsey. No, no, no. This says that you're publisher of Millennial Print.'

'Yeah, that is my job,' Kelsey replies.

Her friend, encouraging Kelsey to take down her job title, retorts: 'It is a great job and I am in constant awe of your accomplishments but this kind of overachieving only works if you're trying to pick up women, all right. Men don't want to deal with your Big Dick Energy.'

Similarly, as I was writing this book, a friend sent me comments from an exchange she'd overheard between a few teenage girls:

'No, you just have to play dumb,' one said.

'Yeah,' another replied. 'Like, if he leaves you on "seen", he had nothing to say back 'cause, like, you're a bit of a know it all.'

From the tender age of sixteen, if not earlier, we seem to be shrinking ourselves. This behaviour has become

a social reflex to a historic power imbalance in relationships. And if we don't stop ourselves from leaning
on it, we are going to slow the progress we are hoping
to speed up.

Claiming Our Little Piece of Earth

While I was writing this book, I found myself watching the Netflix film *Marriage Story*. It stars Scarlett
Johansson and Adam Driver and, as Driver explained in
an interview on *The Late Show with Stephen Colbert*, is
essentially a love story about divorce. It follows a married
couple, Nicole and Charlie, on their journey through the
process of a divorce, portraying how the legal system can
break a couple whose split was amicable, quickly turning
them against each other.

Twenty-five minutes into the film, Nicole is sitting
in the office of divorce attorney Nora (Laura Dern)—
surrounded by fluffy pink pillows and nursing a tea with
Manuka honey—retelling the story of their relationship
in a ten-minute monologue. She was an actress based in
LA, he was an up-and-coming theatre director from New
York, and it was a classic case of infatuation at first sight.
Nicole moved to New York and began starring in Charlie's
theatre shows, and went along with his life—which was

fine in the beginning, because she was the star. But then, the company grew in acclaim and her star faded a little. Then a little more. He was soon the star, and she was in the ensemble. And she started to realise that her sense of herself had been lost in their coupledom; her work (and world) became smaller as his grew bigger. Even having a child—something she thought they could *really* share, but also she could really own—didn't help her find her way back to herself. Nicole continued to shrink and it began to bother her.

'I realised I had never really come alive for myself,' she says. 'I was just feeding his aliveness.'

And then she was offered a starring role in a TV pilot, back in LA.

'It was like this little lifeline thrown to me, *here's this bit of earth that is yours.*' And Charlie's lack of enthusiasm, lack of support, lack of willingness to step back and pass her the ball so that she could have her rightful turn—that was what broke her. 'That's when I realised, he truly didn't see me,' Nicole says. 'He didn't see me as something separate from himself.'

This is such a common narrative—and one that this book aims to change. We are often so terrified that we won't find someone, that when we do fall in love we are consumed with such aliveness and relief that we forget to ask for what we want. We have our own life, and then we meet someone, and it's a slow process of shrinking until we don't know who we are anymore. Or, we shrink ourselves at the start of a relationship out of fear of being penalised, which compromises our ability to be seen as equal—and for our priorities to be seen as equal—once we're in it. So, our world continues to contract.

I do not want you to live in a world, or a relationship, where you shrink yourself and your desires to mold yourself into a man's life only to wake up a decade later to realise you do not have your own little piece of earth, that you are only supporting his. This romantic shift we live in, the tension in Teammate Love, is an environment calling to change this narrative. It is an environment for progress, and one where women can finally step up and demand more. If we are going to wear the statement T-shirts and buy the books and have the expectations; if we truly believe we are only limited by ourselves—we have a role to play in this tug of war. Our job is to pull the rope in the right direction, and in doing so, pull everyone forward. To quote Zadie Smith in *Feel Free* again: 'Progress is never permanent, will always be threatened, must be redoubled, restated and *reimagined* if it is to survive.'

So, as you continue reading this book—this reimagining of progress—know that it asks one favour of you. It asks you to stop shrinking yourself and your desires. It asks you to be yourself and claim your little piece of earth while you fall into a relationship, and then maintain it once you're in one. Because if every single one of us stops shrinking ourselves and walks into every romantic encounter entirely ourselves, men will have no choice but to fully adapt. They will have to step up and accept Teammate Love as the default love in their lives, and we will all be happier for it. It is time for us to recast love on women's terms. And gradually, through the great work of you, your girlfriends, Jacinda Ardern and Beyoncé, we might just be able to run our worlds without romantic compromise. The woman with desires will be entirely desirable.

The favour this book asks of you is unconventional. The majority of mainstream dating books throughout history have encouraged us to play games, to follow rules. To be the confident, independent operator of our professional life but play the subservient role in romantic relationships. To be the mysterious woman, sitting silently in the corner waiting for a man to approach. To avoid making the first move. To wait for him to call. To make ourselves smaller, in every instance, to build up the man in front of us.

They have told us to do this because it works. It is a delicate dance rooted in tradition—one tried, tested and proved to work time and time again. You probably will find a love faster with this approach, you probably will 'attract' more men. But the love these men will give you will not be Teammate Love. It will be a love built on the foundation of tradition, of what is good and bad, right and wrong. It will be Soulmate Love, and this is the love Charlie offered Nicole. It is not Teammate Love. It is not a love with professional respect, and equality, and the rhythm of passing the ball of opportunity between one another at its core. You cannot expect to remain the independent operator of your own life with this love by your side. It is a hand brake. His priorities will always be greater than yours, because you have implied this at the beginning of the dating process. This is an inferior love—and this is not merely my opinion; the research now tells us so.

A wealth of research, which we will explore in Chapter 14, is now showing us that couples with Teammate Love are happier and more satisfied than couples without equality at their core. We see clearly that Teammate Love is now the superior love—and that is what I want for you, for all of us. The best love we can find.

If you find this love, if all of your girlfriends find this love, if all of your male friends find this love, we will all have happier, more satisfied partnerships and happier, more satisfied lives. But collectively, we will do something much bigger. We will create a world where modern professional women are one step closer to only being limited by themselves; a world where they can live their lives entirely free of the dateability penalty; a world where they don't have to shrink themselves in romance; a world where the first question thrown at a woman who holds a powerful seat at the table is not whether she is married and has children; a world where success and love can fully coexist for women, as it already does for men.

But maybe the most beautiful picture I see is this one: a world where the Ruth Bader Ginsburgs of this generation do not have to sit at a Confirmation Hearing and attribute their success to the great good fortune of sharing life with a partner truly extraordinary for his generation. They may not mention him at all. Because if Teammate Love becomes the default love in our lives, the Martys of the world will no longer be extraordinary, but ordinary.

Chapter 3

You Can Make the First Move, but Not Three

When I think about the first move, I think mainly about a subway. It was a cold night in New York City and my girlfriend was heading home. She was a writer at *Cosmopolitan* magazine at the time, so you can probably envisage her life. She was like one of the characters on *The Bold Type*, except she actually had to do some work. She worked long days but was expected to acquire romantic material outside of them, and as she rode home on the subway on this cold night, she saw some in the shape of a handsome man standing across from her. She considered her options until, eventually, her stop approached. She collected her bags and some courage, and pulled out her business card before walking up to him.

'You're beautiful,' she said. 'Here's my number.' With that, the doors opened, and as she stepped onto the platform she heard something behind her.

She looked back to see the entire carriage united in applause.

There is a question that orbits women making the first move, much like the earth orbits the sun. Obviously, women are physically and emotionally capable of approaching a man. We are prime ministers and entrepreneurs and bosses and mothers with moving limbs and working brains making much tougher decisions than whether to lay down our business card in the vicinity of a stranger. The question regards the success rate: we're not sure whether women making the first move actually works.

So much so, when a woman momentarily silences that question in her head to initiate that first contact, the reaction from the outside world isn't one of nonchalance. It's: *'She is brave. She is magnificent.'* We applaud, but only because we don't fully believe it works yet, and that is because of an argument made time and time again.

Evolutionary psychology has told us that men are hunters, therefore women should allow themselves to be hunted. Men are dominant and active, therefore women should be passive. This has taken shape in traditional dating scripts as 'the chase'. Men like to chase; therefore, women should allow men to chase them. By all means, go out and hunt and chase and break the traditional dating scripts in the name of feminism, they say, but it won't work. And no matter how many liberated conversations we spark or nudes we send with nonchalance, we walk around with this argument reverberating in our inner ear, and we exist with a level of anxiety simmering below our romantic lives because we're not sure whether we can successfully take control of them.

I know this because as I walk around telling my girlfriends they are liberated to do whatever they want and demand my internal monologue repeat the same thing, I have never fully believed it. Over the course of writing this book, I have continued to ask the women in my life whether they feel confident to make the first move, and the answer is still conflicted. The majority of women I know in their thirties make the first move, but those in their early twenties are still hesitant. The trend I see focuses on confidence in romance, and indeed in life, or maybe women in their thirties are just fed up and time-poor. Regardless, this hesitation and anxiety exists in women's romantic lives because it's difficult to argue our way around evolutionary psychology. So, in order to resolve it, I went back to the research, which now reveals an entirely different story. One that successfully correlates with the lives of the increasingly liberated women I know.

We Are Shaped by History but We Define the Future

Michael Flood is an Associate Professor at The University of Queensland in the Faculty of Law, School of Justice, and a researcher on men, masculinities, gender and violence prevention. I spoke to Flood extensively about women making the first move, and a wave of relief came over me when he said that social and cultural attitudes now influence women's behaviour (and men's acceptance of this behaviour) more than biology and evolution. In societies that have more gender-equal attitudes, women are more likely to take the initiative in their romantic lives and, as a result, make the first move. Importantly, men are also more likely to accept and respect women making the first move as a viable romantic path. This is evidenced when you look at women's sexual agency—and men's willingness to accept it—across different countries (for example, Saudi Arabia compared to Sweden). But within these societies, it also comes down to the attitude of the individual. 'If you take one thousand women and you survey them on their attitudes towards gender and then the likelihood of women making the first move, again, you see a relationship between those and it's not about biology,' Flood said, 'it's not about evolution. It's about gender norms and gender attitudes.'

When you look at the generations of women in their twenties and thirties across the western world today, you see they are far more likely to make the first move than their mothers and grandmothers. And you also witness a generation of men far more willing to accept a woman's approach. 'What that represents is shifts in gender equality, and shifts, in some ways, towards sexual empowerment,' said Flood. We are on our way, but we are not there yet.

Fortunately, though, there are now new pathways to walk up to the handsome man on the train without *actually* walking up to the handsome man on the train. We can take control of our romantic lives without an audience of applauding strangers and the coinciding fear of public rejection.

How Online Dating Is Shifting the Dial

One night, over cocktails, a twenty-five-year-old marketing executive told a Russian tycoon that she wanted to be in a position where a guy didn't have her number, but she had his. Recalling the conversation later for *Forbes* magazine, she said, 'What if women make the first move, send the first message? And if they don't, the match disappears after twenty-four hours, like in Cinderella, the pumpkin and the carriage? . . . What if we could hardwire that into a product?' For the record, the Russian tycoon had her number. In fact, she had flown from her home base of Austin, Texas, to his home base in London more than fifteen times in the past three months. They'd spent days walking and talking along London's streets and parks before arriving at this night, with these cocktails, where they stumbled upon a billion-dollar idea that would become a company with unicorn status. The woman was Whitney Wolfe Herd, the Russian tycoon was Andrey Andreev, and the idea is now the fastest-growing dating app in the United States: Bumble.

Since Bumble launched in 2014, more than 1.5 billion first moves have been made by women, and most recently, 25 million matches made per week. While they are unable to provide exact numbers on romantic relationships formed, they can confirm that more than 20,000 marriages and engagements began from a mutual right swipe on Bumble. And with each successful relationship formed as a result of a woman making the first move, the evolutionary argument claiming women cannot take their dating life into their own hands because men are hunters and women must be hunted is slowly being made redundant.

But online dating, as a whole, has also been beneficial for women in an unexpected way. While it is a pain in the backside because it is so transactional, it is phenomenal *because* it is so transactional. We have been brought up to believe that men are the initiators, but many studies show that women actually make the first move—just not in the way we might assume. Women do this not so much by walking over to a man at the bar and cracking a corny one-liner, but by indicating to the man across the bar that he can walk over to her and crack a corny one-liner. Women do this with a look. You know that look. You've seen that look. You've given that look. It's the beginning of the flirtatious exchange, and it is also what these studies consider the first move, indicating interest.

What dating apps have done is take all these men and women located in the bar and place them in an equal space where they can swipe right to indicate interest. Thus swiping right replaces the approach, it replaces the look. And women are quite happy to swipe right first, because they have been doing it for eternity anyway, just not on their phones. In doing so, these apps are creating a place for women to feel comfortable swiping right because there is only one first move to make. The look and the corny one-liner equal the same action: swiping right.

However, when it comes to Bumble—where only women can make the first move, and men must respond to them within twenty-four hours otherwise their connection disappears—a place has been created where women not only feel liberated to make the first move, but confident in doing so. It puts *more* power in women's hands. And when women are more confident, when they feel they can take control in a situation, when they believe they have more power, research shows they are more likely to make the first move.

A study conducted by the University of Waterloo's Jennifer MacGregor and Columbia University's Justin Cavallo in 2011 argued that social expectations discouraged women from pursuing men and instead encouraged them to use passive strategies to find and form relationships, so the researchers investigated whether they could manipulate the sense of control a woman felt when initiating a relationship. Researchers asked the participants to recall either high personal-control conditions or low personal-control conditions. As expected, women's intention to initiate a relationship peaked under high personal-control conditions; it was even equal to men's. For women, just recalling a moment of high personal-control seemed to counteract all the dating rule books that for decades have instructed them to remain passive in romance. So, in conditions where women feel more personal control—such as Bumble—they are comfortable making the first move, and as a result, more women are successful.

It is my hope that eventually, through the millions of first moves and millions of successful first moves, we will reach a point where a woman handing a man her business card in a subway carriage will not be greeted with a round of applause. You will be liberated to make as many corny one-liners as you please without being told you are *brave* and *magnificent*. You will just be doing something normal.

However, if you're concerned that your strike rate will not be as high as your Uber rating, know this: it may not be. You may be successful seventeen times, and unsuccessful three. You may be unsuccessful more times than you are successful. But the point isn't a 100 per cent success rate, or 4.74 stars in corny one-liners. The point is having a choice, and the ability to choose that damn choice whenever you damn well choose to.

One of the finest definitions of feminism I have encountered is from author and journalist Caitlin Moran, who told *Future Women* that feminism is 'the belief that women should be allowed to be as nuts, fat, dim, deluded, and lacklustre as men, on exactly their same pay-scale'. She continued: 'I don't want women to aspire to succeed if it means having to be groundbreakingly excellent. That's exhausting. I want us to aspire to just getting away with the bare minimum, like the ho-hum dudes currently sitting in the chairs of power. That's true equality.' And just like the mediocre men dominating boardrooms and bars, you deserve to be just as average, to approach men with as many corny pick-up lines as you please. It's not about being good at it. It's about having the right to play in the arena—and possibly be terrible. Because we have forgotten something: the men who approach us are often entirely useless at it. They resort to negging or backing into you on the dancefloor and then pretending it was an accident. Or, sometimes they are perfectly skilled at it but still fail because there are other factors at play.

I was once at a bar recovering from being dumped by a man from a particular football club. Men from that particular football club were also at this bar, and one of them took a liking to me and made me aware of it. He told me I was beautiful and asked whether he could buy me a drink. I said no. He asked why. I said it was because he played for this particular football club. He said he didn't. I said he did. He asked me how I knew. I explained he was wearing a T-shirt with the football club's logo on it. He looked down at his shirt and probably thought, *Shit*. His failed attempt had nothing to do with his approach, but my attitude, and probably his sartorial choices that day.

We can't live with hesitation or fear of taking the initiative in our romantic lives, because half the time we have no control over the outcome anyway. Feeling like we have to perform or manipulate a situation only reinforces this and hands over more power to men. So, have a go and possibly be terrible at it. Whitney Wolfe Herd has given you the golden ticket. But before you arm yourself with a catalogue of shitty pick-up lines, arm yourself with the following golden guideline as well.

You Can Only Make the First Move Once

The first thing you need to know about making the first move is you can only make it once. Not twice. Not three times. When you make the first move, you've laid your cards of interest on the table and the person you approached can see them very clearly. They can. Truly. It's not a matter of them not seeing them, or not being able to read them. They can see them *and* read them. They can either respond to your cards or ignore them. So, if you make the first move and a guy chooses to ignore your cards, do not put more on the table. He has chosen to ignore them for one of two reasons: 1) he's not interested, or 2) he doesn't like women making the first move.

Now, both of these reasons are perfectly fine. In fact, they are great. If he's not interested, why would you want to date him? Because he looks like Brad Pitt? Fair enough. (I was going to use Leonardo DiCaprio here, but a small poll decided Brad Pitt has aged better.) But do you know where you'll probably arrive if you make the second and third moves and Brad Pitt finally gives in?

Heartbreak. Because Brad Pitt isn't interested in you. He either feels obliged or is entertaining the idea with the probable motive of casual sex. And after one or two dates, once he gets what he wants or doesn't, he'll probably let you down politely and depart the situation. That is the first scenario.

Here is the second. If Brad Pitt* isn't saying yes to your first move because he doesn't like women making the first move, you definitely don't want to make the second and third moves. Because if he finally gives in, he will not be an evolved man with progressive views of women and their place in the world. If he doesn't accept you taking control of your dating life he probably won't be the man who respects your desires and sees them as equal to his in the future. 'If, when a woman makes the first move, that man rejects it because he finds her too sexually agentic, then I think that's a red flag that he's going to be a poor partner,' Michael Flood said. 'A man who is resistant or hostile to women's initiative is also, I think, making himself a poor partner.' And, if through some Tarantino-esque miracle you end up with Brad Pitt, he will probably continue to see his needs and ambitions as greater than yours through the course of your relationship.

* I'm sure Brad Pitt loves and respects women. This was maybe a terrible analogy.

By making the first move, you liberate yourself. You rule out the guys who don't really like you and the guys who can't offer up Teammate Love. By making the second move and third moves, you risk either ending up with someone who doesn't really want to be with you and is likely to let you down, or you will arrive at a place even worse than this: in a relationship with a man who does not appreciate a woman as his equal and will definitely not give you Teammate Love.

The Cost of Avoiding the First Move

If, as young women, we live in fear of making the first move, if we doubt ourselves as we attempt to take control of our romantic lives, we are more likely to enter less fulfilling, less gender-equal relationships.

'It's true that if a woman routinely waits for men to make the first move, waits for men to initiate the relationship, waits for men to initiate sexual activity and progress through sexual activity and so on,' Flood said. 'Then I think it's likely that will be a poorer relationship. Because, by definition, it's a relationship where one person's needs are not being expressed and not therefore being heard.'

This does not mean you must make the first move in every romantic relationship. Making the first move is not the defining condition for Teammate Love. But if you walk through romance with limited sexual agency, you risk entering an unequal relationship because you are silently implying that a man's needs and desires are greater than yours. So, make the first move when you like, and apply the Bumble approach to your entire dating life. If you make the first move, he has one opportunity to lay his cards of interest on the table and spark up conversation. If he doesn't, you and your interest disappear. It's a simple strategy you can work within, and therefore have confidence in. You don't need to overthink, or perform, or hesitate, which only increases women's anxiety around relationships and indirectly hands over more power to men. So, go work on those shitty pick-up lines. Time to lay them down, terribly, and see where they land.

Chapter 4

Get the Bill

For a good year, my boyfriend and I consoled my sister about her work. She was considering a career change, as we all do after completing the first degree only to realise we were never really interested in it in the first place. Anyway, she had finished the degree and was now sitting in a job that had allowed her to move cities and meet fascinating people, but it was in neither the industry she was interested in nor the realm of her first degree. She was stuck, like Malcolm, in the middle. Not knowing how she had arrived here and how to get where she wanted to go. But she had an idea. So, every now and then, when the path to this new career seemed too steep or a road-block appeared, when she doubted whether she should run up it at all, our counselling sessions occurred.

During one such session, money was the roadblock. She was twenty-four, and to reach this new career she would have to return to study and watch her HECS debt climb a little higher. And as all twenty-four-year-olds believe at twenty-four, she thought it was far too late to change. She only had approximately seven decades left of her life, and as she sat trying to talk herself out of losing more money to enter a career she would probably love for the next seven decades, she thought she had missed the boat. It was gone. She was stuck here, forever, on the dock of unfulfillment watching her boat sail into the horizon. Until my boyfriend said, 'Esther, it's not about the money!' She looked him square in the face, appearing to take it in and nodded, before turning to me and whispering: '*It's about the money.*'

Ever since that counselling session, when an appropriate moment appears, we chime, 'It's not about the money! *It's about the money,*' because it's a fun joke. She knows it. She's since slid into that new career path and fortunately for her, it's been worth it—and that is what we are here to talk about. What is worth money and what money is worth. As we live in a capitalistic society, money holds a certain value. And while you choose what you do with it, money is never free, so your dinner isn't either. And to explain this overly simplistic argument, I am about to take you on an imaginary one. Because it's not about the money! *It's about the money.*

It's 9.05pm on a Thursday. You're on your first date with Blake. He's a Creative Director at a branding agency, you've learned, with an interest in foreign films and Persian cats. You've spent ninety-seven minutes bonding over your mutual appreciation of Persians but the fun has been interrupted by the bill arriving. Blake rummages around in his pocket for his wallet. He locates it, opens it, pulls out his card and looks up. You're sitting there quietly on your phone, killing time scrolling Instagram. He cops the bill for the evening. And as he does, Blake is making an assumption about you while you sit there quietly scrolling. Because your silence actually says something very loud.

I can be bought.

Now, before you roll your eyes, claim chivalry is not entirely dead and suggest we capitalise on the final remnants of it, I would argue we shouldn't. Because if anyone is losing, it is you.

By allowing someone else to pay for your date, you are saying your time and romantic interest can be purchased at a price—a two-course dinner and a median-range bottle of wine—and that is a tricky path to wander. Not only because it's a relatively cheap price tag, but because you're laying down unequal ground on which to build a relationship. You become the seller, and Blake the buyer. And if you don't believe you are selling your romantic interest, you are saying something else: that your time is worth more than Blake's, and therefore he must pay for it. Either way, your economic arrangement has been established. You trade your time and company for money. And that will be the ongoing arrangement throughout your relationship, if you don't change it quickly. If you continue this economic arrangement, it can become a very slippery slope.

Enter, a brief interlude depicting where this could go.

The Shortcut

In life, for some women, there is an easy route. The young, beautiful woman allows herself to be snapped up by a wealthy suitor, bears the children, takes on the unpaid work at home or supervises the nanny, and lives a life upgraded on her husband's black Amex. It's called 'the shortcut', and in a way it's possibly the fastest route to achieving wealth as a young woman. On this route, men become ATMs. As long as you remain beautiful and youthful, the ATM will continue dispensing cash. That trade-off is your economic arrangement. But there's a catch. Your part of the deal, well, that becomes a tough gig as the years go by. Fortunately there's botox, but unfortunately there aren't many detours on this path of reliance you've chosen to wander. So, before you merrily trot down it, let's take a deeper look.

In October 2007, in New York City, a young, beautiful woman turned to Craigslist to ponder why she couldn't find a man who a) earned an annual salary of at least half a million dollars and b) wanted to marry her. She labelled herself an 'enterprising young woman' and reiterated that half a million a year was classified middle class in the city, so she really wasn't asking for much. She was in her mid-twenties (tick!), spectacularly beautiful (tick!), could match any man in culture (tick!), was able to keep a nice home (tick!), hearth (relevancy?) and exuded sophistication (debatable). As Alicia Keys had told her, New York City was the concrete jungle where dreams are made, and hers were yet to materialise. What was she doing wrong? She didn't know, and she wanted to give Alicia Keys the benefit of the doubt, so she asked Craigslist.

A businessman quickly came to the rescue, but not in the way she had hoped. He explained, in pure business terms, that she was a depreciating asset and he would not, as a result, take her 'crappy business deal'. She would bring her looks to the table and he would bring his money—but the problem was that her looks would fade as she aged while his wealth would continue to grow—likely exponentially. In economic terms, he was an appreciating asset while she was a depreciating one. 'So in Wall Street terms, we would call you a trading position, not a buy and hold—hence the rub—marriage,' the businessman wrote. 'It doesn't make good business sense to "buy you" (which is what you're asking) so I'd rather lease.'

While you're likely thinking this is pretty cruel, he makes an excellent—and fair—defence. If his money disappeared, it's likely this woman would too. So, if her beauty fades, he needs an 'out'. The deal he proposed was to date, instead of marry. But before signing off on Craigslist, he made a separate, but also useful, point. 'I find it hard to believe that if you are as gorgeous as you say you are that the $500K hasn't found you, if not only for a tryout,' he wrote. 'By the way, you could always find a way to make your own money and then we wouldn't need to have this difficult conversation.'

And therein lies the kicker. Put your half of the money on the table, and you remove the need for this difficult conversation. Your economic arrangement automatically shifts back to equal ground, and though your shared path may not have black Amex cards and gold frequent-flyer status, it will be all the sweeter for its self-reliance and mutual respect.

The Value of Fifty

Let's return to dinner with Blake. Your riveting Persian cat discourse has been interrupted by the waiter plonking the bill down on the table. Blake is rummaging around in his pocket. He locates his wallet, opens it, pulls out his card and looks up. You're leaning over the table, putting your card on the bill. 'Let's split it down the middle,' you say and lean back.

He will say one of two things: 'You sure?' as he puts his card on top of yours, or, 'No, I insist,' as he puts his card down, pushing yours off the plate. And both of those options are fine. If he insists, let him shout this one but you should mentally pocket that fifty dollars and spend it on him somewhere else. Maybe you shout the nightcaps, or you add it to the imaginary tab in your head and next week, on your second date with Blake, you add that fifty dollars to the next meal, which only makes it easier to shout the entire dinner. And you continue going one for one. If he doesn't let you, employ stealth and pay the bill on your way to the bathroom. In the end, it's about arriving at fifty/fifty where you can, but if you're meeting resistance, it's about the value of fifty dollars. Above all, it's the gesture that matters.

If All Else Fails, Be Polite

British dating coach, writer and YouTube star Matthew Hussey was once asked by an audience member at an event who should get the bill, and his response made an excellent point about what putting your card on the table conveys to a man on the first date. 'If you go on a date with a guy and you don't offer to pay your share, you weren't taught right. If you go on a date and he doesn't pay, he wasn't taught right,' he said, his response later broadcast via YouTube. 'I can tell you right now, if I was dating someone and they never offered to pay, I wouldn't be dating them because this is the most polite they're ever going to be and they're not even trying to pay now.'

When you go on a first date, you put effort into your outfit and your general appearance and attempt to make sure your energy levels are in a decent place so you won't be less than average company. You put all this effort into being your best that evening and then you throw in the towel when the bill arrives by not reaching for your purse? It doesn't make sense. You want to be the very best version of yourself on the first date, and that includes paying your share. It doesn't just remove the risk of entering an unequal relationship, it begins it with a kind gesture that says, *You, across the table from me, are worth my time and I had a nice time.* Even if you had a terrible time, put your money on the table, because you can walk away knowing you were polite.

Would you go to dinner with your girlfriends and not put your card on the table when the bill arrived? No, you wouldn't, because you probably wouldn't have friends for much longer. So, treat the person opposite you now as you would a good friend. 'I would always treat my partner as I would treat my best friend, and I wouldn't apply a different standard to my partner than my best friend,' Hussey said in the same video. 'I wouldn't say to my best friend, "Let's always go out to dinner and you always pay." I'd say, "Let's be teammates here in whatever way we can."'

And the Martys, the men out there offering Teammate Love, will be impressed when you get the bill. They will recognise your polite gesture and they will look across the table and see a woman who will be an equal partner, not something to own.

Contribute What You Can, and Live Within Both Your Means

Once you're beyond the first date, and a few months in, the black-and-white of getting the bill does merge into shades of grey. You and Blake may have similar earning capacities because he is a Creative Director and you are in finance, or you may have vastly different earning capacities because Blake is a Creative Director and you are a writer. If Blake wants to take you out to an expensive dinner beyond your means, contribute what is fair comparatively. For example, you may earn a quarter of his salary, so contribute to a quarter of the dinner. And to maintain balance, ensure you choose the next dinner venue and find one within your budget.

If the relationship evolves into something serious, it does require a conversation and finding a solution that works for both of you. This solution will be different for every couple, but the end goal is the same. At its core it's about living within both of your means to ensure you both continue to see *both* of your salaries as essential and *both* of your professional lives as equal and valid. For many couples, they eventually commit to more expensive life choices because the person earning the higher salary wants them and can afford them, so the couple begins to view this person's salary as essential and the other person's as expendable. The latter is not always, but statistically more often, the woman's career and salary. So, once you get past the initial first few dates, and into a territory where you understand each other's situations, prioritise living within both of your means to ensure both of your careers are seen as equal and no one's takes priority. It starts with fifty dollars, and ends with your willingness to sometimes have a difficult conversation.

Chapter 5

You're Too Cool

I was going to mention Kanye West, until I remembered a lot of people don't like Kanye West. I am a people pleaser, you see, but the problem is that the people are often pleased by very different things. So, it gets tricky. Trying to please everyone only leads you to one place: disappointing yourself. Or the only place worse than that: not being yourself. Which is a dangerous place to dance in.

We live in an era of likes and gratification and cancel culture and public humiliation, which only makes it more difficult to be yourself. But when I was four, it wasn't. When I was four, I was very much myself. I had worn dresses up until that point but at four, I was done. I had trees to climb and monkey bars to swing, which called for one thing: pants. I wore pants up until high school when I probably lost myself again or the school uniform denied them and ever since then, I've been climbing me, myself and my character back to pants. I have dabbled in skirts and dresses, both short and long, but as I tinker on the edge of my late twenties I am back in the good place, which, for me, is wearing pants. For as long as I have thought about it (which is a lot) I am still lost as to why pants are so good. They are comfortable. I know that. But I do not know why they are so good. They just are.

Pants are the closest metaphor I can find to describe being yourself. Because being yourself doesn't require explaining either. It just *is*. You just *are*. But as we grow up into adults and are defined by our jobs and Instagram bios and the crowd around us, we are more often than not shaped by the collective expectations of these surroundings. If we're not changed by these expectations entirely, we often put a temporary mask on to meet them. For women dancing in the dating arena, this mask is usually called The Cool Girl. See, The Cool Girl is the manifestation of our perceived assumption of what men want. And it leaves us in one place: exhausted.

The Cool Girl and Her Window Dressing

If you're not acquainted with The Cool Girl, let me introduce you to Amy Elliott Dunne, the character created by Gillian Flynn in her bestselling novel *Gone Girl*. Amy Elliott Dunne described The Cool Girl early on in the novel and her description has stayed in my mind ever since. The Cool Girl, she said, was always hot and smart and witty and adored football. She didn't care if men burped or told dirty jokes. She probably told them too. She had a model physique while jamming hotdogs and hamburgers into her mouth, followed by her palate cleanser of choice, cheap beer. She didn't care about her calorie count or—maybe most importantly—what the man she was dating did. 'Cool Girls are above all hot. Hot and understanding,' Amy wrote, accurately distilling the woman we can all play. 'Cool Girls never get angry; they only smile in a chagrined, loving manner and let their men do whatever they want. Go ahead, shit on me, I don't mind, I'm the Cool Girl.'

Now, it is fun jamming hot dogs and hamburgers into your mouth. It is fun drinking cheap beer and adoring football and being carelessly thin while having the appetite of a forty-two-year-old father of three. It is fun telling dirty jokes and never getting angry. Until it isn't. Because it was never really fun in the first place, was it? It was a role you played because the cost of all of the aforementioned actions was outweighed by the reward of spending time with the guy you like. Until eventually, the cost did not outweigh the reward, because you grew used to his company.

The problem with being The Cool Girl is that it is an act. An excellent act that is perceived to be successful, but I would argue it isn't. It is successful in the short term, but an entirely useless performance if you reshape your entire personality to play it. The act is designed to lure him in, but it does not result in a compatible relationship, because eventually he will realise the woman he signed up for does not like jamming hot dogs and hamburgers into her mouth, does not drink cheap beer and adore football, and he will be confused. Because you said you were. But you are not. Because you were not being yourself. You were being what you thought he wanted you to be. And eventually, you could not uphold the act anymore, whether that was three months in or three years in. The relationship will now have changed because you have changed, back to the real you, and if the real you is not compatible with him, unlike The Cool Girl was, there will, of course, be problems.

If you like jamming hotdogs into your mouth and you love football, great. You are being yourself and you will keep doing all of the above when you're in this relationship because it is easy. It just *is*. You just *are*. You walked into the courting process wearing pants and once you're committed, for lack of a better metaphor, you're still wearing pants. But if you walk in wearing skirts and after some period of time can't bear it anymore and switch back to wearing pants, he will be confused. And when you enter a relationship with a person only to wake up one morning to find another version of that person facing you, it is fairly unlikely this relationship will keep working. Because the dynamic has shifted. The compatibility has shifted. Your behaviour has shifted. Because it was exhausting playing someone you're not.

Let me provide a more literal example. Let's say you walk into an interview for a sales manager role at a tech company. You believe your future employer will want an outgoing personality in the role, so you walk in and act. You become the most outgoing person possible for thirty-seven minutes, selling them someone you are definitely not but can maintain for thirty-seven minutes, and then you walk out to fall in a heap—and next week answer the phone to hear you've got the job. You have to walk in one month later, and be that person again, for eight hours a day, five days a week, and you wake up six months later, burnt out. You can't do it anymore. So, you put your pants back on and walk in every day following this breakdown, being yourself, which you know is not what they want. They don't, and eventually you don't meet your KPIs and they fire you. Well, that went swimmingly.

So, why do we walk into the first date and pretend to be someone we're not, to win the courting process but enter a relationship that is not real? That is not fair on him and not fair on you. But the larger issue I have with it, is this: Why would you waste everybody's time? There are so many people in this world you have the opportunity to connect with and you're choosing to fake it only to enter a relationship and arrive at a destination that probably won't work for you, or him, because you were never yourself to start with.

So, what do you do? You take your pants and you put them back on and you walk into every first date as yourself. If you love hotdogs and hamburgers and football, excellent. Be that. Do that. If you don't, excellent. Be everything other than that. Everything that is You.

Because the reality is, it is very difficult to please everyone. As I said six pages ago, the problem with pleasing the people is that the people are often pleased by very different things. And this is the caveat to The Cool Girl. There are, as Amy once said, 'variations to the window dressing'. 'Maybe he's a vegetarian, so Cool Girl loves seitan and is great with dogs; or maybe he's a hipster artist, so Cool Girl is a tattooed, bespectacled nerd who loves comics.' So, in order to be The Cool Girl you have to make an assumption about this man you are dating, and another assumption about what version of The Cool Girl you should play in order to please him. You have not only made one assumption, but two. And assumptions, more often than not, are incorrect and, hence, unreliable. Because they are assumptions.

Let me take you back to our literal example. You are back at the job interview. Actually, you are sitting in the hallway waiting to walk into the job interview. And as you sit there, waiting, you run back through your mind what you *think* they want. You *think* they want outgoing, they want loud, they want extroverted. So, you harness every cell of your extroversion and as they call your name, you walk that extroversion in and perform. Thirty-seven minutes later you leave, exhausted, but you have nailed it. And one week later you receive a call. Someone else got the job. You weren't quite what they were looking for.

Unfortunately, while you were in there performing, your possible future employer was sitting there knowing exactly what they were looking for: an introverted big thinker who could quietly lead the team and take control of the sales strategy because they had just read Susan Cain's bestselling book *Quiet*, which argues that introverts make better leaders, and they had no introverts in this team. Meanwhile, you, an introverted big thinker, missed the role because you were too busy pretending you were some-one you were not. When, in fact, they were looking for you. And they missed you. All because you made an assumption.

Don't Make Assumptions

Don Miguel Ruiz is a Mexican author whose most acclaimed book, *The Four Agreements*, explains how four agreements or rules can liberate humans to live freer, easier lives. One of those agreements is 'Don't Make Assumptions'.

Ruiz believes we assume everyone feels the way we do, and if we don't approve of ourselves, we believe others will not approve of who we are. 'And this is why we have a fear of being ourselves around others,' he sagely writes. 'Because we think everyone else will judge us, victimize us, abuse us, and blame us as we do ourselves. So even before others have a chance to reject us, we have already rejected ourselves.'

This is why it is so hard, sometimes, to wear pants and be ourselves, because quite often we don't approve of who we really are. But it is not your job to decide what the person before you wants and approves. It is up to them. And it is unfair to make that decision for them, by not showing them who you truly are. They are missing out and so are you. You wouldn't want the man you are dating to present an entirely different version of himself because he assumed that's the version you wanted. You want the opportunity to get to know him, and see whether you're compatible. Give him the same opportunity.

Be the Maximum Version of Your Character

In an interview with David Letterman, Kanye West told the story of his friend, who advised him that his power was his influence. He looked at his friend, thought about it for a moment, and disagreed. 'My power is the ability *not* to be influenced,' he said.

It left Letterman speechless, which is fair, because it also left me fairly silent. Now, whether or not you like Kanye West is not the point. The point is that there is power in *not* being influenced—in life generally, but particularly when it comes to dating. If you walk through your romantic life focusing on what other people want, you lose time and energy you could instead spend figuring out what *you* want.

Being the maximum version of yourself is a political act in a world where women continue to shrink themselves to build up or appease the men in front of them. The action states that you, and your desires, are just as important as the man before you while also providing you both with an opportunity to see whether you, your values, and your lives are compatible. And if they are, it's likely the man before you will love and respect the fact that you have been yourself from the beginning. In this modern existence, where our lives are performed on social media only to be gratified with daily metrics, it is not just rare but refreshing to see people be themselves in the face of rejection. As Kanye West said in the Letterman interview, 'I love people being the maximum version of their character. I love people being themselves.'

So, from the first date to the seventeenth, be strong enough to be yourself. Do not be so influenced by the presence of the man before you that you quietly mold yourself into another version in order to please him, especially when he hasn't asked you to. The small, consistent act of *not* being influenced holds a quiet power.

What appears to be the scariest part of this process is in fact the most liberating part of the process. Being yourself, and not being influenced by external factors, does the work for you, because you show up, day one, and every day after that, showing the person on the other side of the table exactly who you are. And they will either like it or they won't. Just as you will like them or you won't. Just as you like Kanye West or you don't. Do you think he cares? Not really.

So, go out there and be the maximum version of your character and it will sort the men you connect with from the men you don't connect with. And it will sort something else for you. It will sort Teammate Love from every other love. Because the man who accepts you for who you are, and loves you for who you are, is the man who will also respect you. Why would you pretend to be someone else to later arrive, exhausted, at a love any less than Teammate Love?

The 'I Hope I Like Him' Principle

There is a common mindset that women often walk into first—and usually second, and third—dates with: *I hope he likes me.* The very performance of The Cool Girl says

I hope he likes me. As you put on your makeup, as you sit in the Uber, as you walk to the venue, your mind has a tornado twirling *I hope he likes me, I hope he likes me, I hope he likes me* around in it, momentarily destroying whatever else had priority in there.

I know this because it has often twirled around in my mind, and as countless flatmates have walked out the door saying, 'I hope he likes me,' I have often stopped them and replied, 'No. I hope *you* like *him*.' And that is what we must do for ourselves whenever The Cool Girl begins to creep in with her destructive words. Whenever we begin thinking *I hope he likes me*, we must repeat the antidote—*I hope I like him*—to ourselves as we put on our makeup, as we sit in the Uber, and as we walk to the venue. It does not just momentarily quell any anxieties about the situation, it repositions our focus in the right direction: toward ourselves.

We are not dating to win a likeability contest, but to find someone we can share Teammate Love with. Right now, in this moment, it is about *your* life, not theirs. Maybe it will be about your life together eventually, but right now, have your own back. The man you are about to meet is perfectly capable of having his—and he will—so take care of your own interests. Walking into each romantic encounter thinking *I hope I like him* reminds you that you are actually in control of the situation, you have equal power, and this is about what you want as much as it is about what he wants.

This mindset flows on to your behaviour in any romantic encounter and allows you to be the maximum version of your character with greater ease. It provides you with more opportunities to express your values and interests and discover whether the values of the man before you are in line with yours. It encourages you to work out *what you want*, but, crucially, reminds you that *what you want* is not only valid, but the most important thing at this date. Time to serve it.

Chapter 6

Know What You Want, and Talk About It

When I think about the word 'adaptation', I think, mainly, about myself. I am a chronic adapter. This is a problem and an ability I am now actively trying to curtail, and one I associate closely with people pleasing. I blame mostly my parents here. I was raised in a household where being nice, being polite, was the currency we traded in public. If you spilled your oat-milk latte on me, I would probably apologise for you. I am *that nice*. But I am not really *that nice*. I just behave *that nice* in public because that is apparently what I'm supposed to do. I will talk politics or culture depending on who I am in a room with. I can be an old soul or a young idiot depending on my company. I read the room and I adapt in order to make other people feel more comfortable. It is not something I am proud of, but Dale Carnegie would be. I will ensure everyone is comfortable and content and getting along, often at my own expense. Because I am *that nice*. And in the process, I often lose my sense of self and return home feeling like I've just stepped out of a tumble dryer with a case of disorientated selfhood. I don't know who I am anymore. *Am I serious? Am I fun? Am I none?* I forget, so I write it down, and then I re-enter the world to do it all over again.

I blame mostly my parents for this chronic adaptation, when I really shouldn't blame them. They are nice parents, kind parents, loving parents. And they are the parents who raised three daughters in a world where girls are meant to play nice. They are meant to *be nice*. Because nice girls are likeable girls and likeable girls go far in this world.

My parents simply wanted us to survive.

Adaptation is defined as the process of change that helps an organism or species become better suited to its environment. And for centuries women have been socialised to be the nurturer, the homemaker, the wife, the permanent supporter cheering their husband—their breadwinner—on from the sidelines. Women, through-out time, have consistently adapted themselves to fit this brief, to better suit the environment around them. As a result, we have developed traits such as kind-ness and compassion and care—which were, and still are, valued most in women. And since we secured the right to vote, the right to work, the right to own our own homes and bodies and lives, cultural notions of what make 'good' traits in 'good' women lag behind.

The kind, caring woman still gets ahead, receiving the gold star of public approval. However, it only gets her so far. This archetype makes it harder for her to evolve beyond this, so she maintains her status as a chronic adapter while centuries-old tropes around evolution and gender still stick.

In 2018, newly minted New Zealand Prime Minister Jacinda Ardern announced she was pregnant and went on to give a new face to power, showing the world motherhood and power could, in fact, coexist. One year earlier, the Pew Research Center sat down 4573 Americans and asked them what traits they valued most in men and women. They were asked to list three adjectives to describe how men and women should and shouldn't be. In an age where girls are growing up with books telling them they can be anything in this world, and witnessing women like Ardern govern countries, you would think these answers would be less gendered, more evolved. But they were not.

The questionnaire revealed positive attributes for a woman included 'beauty', 'kindness', 'compassion' and 'responsibility'. While for men, positive words included 'strong', 'powerful' and 'ambitious'. Negative attributes in women included 'ambitious' and 'masculine', and the word 'powerful' was a particularly controversial one. Ninety-two per cent of respondents said that a woman should not be powerful, while 67 per cent said a man should. And when it came to a woman's 'independence', the results were conflicted: 51 per cent said independence was a trait women should have, while 49 per cent argued it was a trait they shouldn't. The word 'provider' was also only used to describe men, not women.

In an age where women are leading countries and companies and their own lives, the world is still divided on whether our independence and power is a positive thing. And when young men are conditioned to believe these stereotypes, it trickles on into the rest of our lives, including sometimes our romantic lives. We suffer a likeability penalty in both the workplace and modern romance—and finding Teammate Love only becomes more difficult, yet all the more crucial.

The Likeability Penalty

Back in 2013, Facebook's chief operating officer Sheryl Sandberg, who has spent a good half a decade telling women to *lean in*, wrote in her book of the same name that natural-born female leaders suffer a likeability penalty. This is a penalty that begins early on in the sandpit. 'When a little boy asserts himself, he's called a "leader",' Sandberg wrote a year later. 'Yet when a little girl does the same, she risks being branded "bossy".

Words like bossy send a message: don't speak up. By middle school, girls are less interested in leading than boys—a trend that continues into adulthood.'

Sandberg argues that women in the workplace face social penalties for behaving in a way that leads to power and success, while men do not. And it puts us in a tricky predicament, which the famous case of Heidi Roizen may have summed up best.

Heidi Roizen is a successful Silicon Valley venture capitalist who was the subject of a 2003 study conducted by then Columbia Business School professor Francis Flynn and then New York University professor Cameron Anderson. They presented students with two CVs, which were identical except for one detail. Half the students were presented with the name 'Heidi Roizen' at the top of the CV, while the other half received the same CV belonging to 'Howard Roizen'. What followed was one of the finest illustrations of the likeability penalty in action. When asked who they would prefer to work with, the students overwhelmingly voted for Howard, who was considered vastly more appealing than Heidi. The students rated Heidi and Howard equally competent, but Heidi came across as 'selfish', and 'not the type of person you would want to hire or work for'. The exact same CV, completely different results caused by the simple change of a name.

Actress Marlo Thomas may have summed it up best in her memoir *Growing Up Laughing*: 'A man has to be Joe McCarthy to be called ruthless. All a woman has to do is put you on hold.'

The pool of successful, educated women affected by this likeability penalty is larger than ever, and as the likeability penalty swiftly evolves into the dateability penalty, the smart, successful woman continues to be penalised in her romantic life as well. So, she takes this discrimination and adapts; and as we saw in Chapter 2, she shrinks herself and her desires in the hope of finding a great love.

Some of the most ambitious, educated and successful women on the planet have been known to shrink themselves. As we saw in Chapter 2, even single women who were elite MBA students tried to avoid appearing 'too ambitious, assertive, or pushy' in front of men. They reported lower desired salaries, said they would work fewer hours, and rated themselves with lower professional ambition and leadership qualities than they truly believed. But, it was only the single women who tended to shrink themselves and their ambitions; not the women in relationships, or men at all.

Historically, women have been socialised to believe that our professional ambition is not an asset but a roadblock in romance. But now it is not. At least not to a significant portion of men, and those are the men who have the potential to offer Teammate Love. While the women of RBG's time had to talk themselves down to survive, you do not. In fact, talking yourself down is now only supporting the dateability penalty and preventing Teammate Love arriving in your life. So, what do we need to do? We take our ambition and success and flip the perceived problem on its head to sort the men who admire and respect successful women, from the men who do not. Now, when we find ourselves in chronic adapter mode, when we start shrinking ourselves, we snap ourselves out of it and we do the exact opposite. We take our story, and we own it.

The Power in Owning Your Story, and Claiming Your Little Piece of Earth

In her memoir, *Becoming*, Michelle Obama wrote that one of the most useless questions an adult can ask a child is what they want to be when they grow up. 'As if growing up is finite,' she sagely wrote. 'As if at some point you become something and that is the end.'

You probably did not know what you wanted to be when you were twelve, and even if you did, you are likely to have changed your mind eleven times over. And this is absolutely fine, because there is this thing called life we are forced to adapt to and evolve with and as we live, we grow, and therefore change, many times over. All you know at the age of twelve is who you have grown into over those twelve years and what that person likes. You do not know exactly where you want to go or who you want to be but you know you have the ambition to go *somewhere*. So, you take your ambition and you run. You keep running, until one day you wake up to realise you've arrived somewhere—and you can look back as well as forward. When that moment arrives, you have a story. That story is not over but it has begun.

And this is where we arrive at another thing Michelle Obama and I agree on: the necessity to own your story. Because there is a power in this story, if you give it power. 'Even when it's not pretty or perfect. Even when it's more real than you want it to be. Your story is what you have, what you will always have,' Obama wrote. 'It is something to own.' If you don't own it, someone else will and you will no longer hold this power. They will.

When I was five, I signed a contract. It was a very serious evening in the bubble bath and the discussion was heated. I am not baptised and so I don't have a godmother, but I was with the equivalent of my godmother that night. It was her bath, but my bubbles, and our conversation had become quite serious. I hadn't really warmed to babies. I didn't want to have them, but she kept saying I would one day, after I married my husband. But I wasn't really into husbands either. So, I asked her to fetch me a document. She returned with a serviette and a pen, and because I was five the equivalent of my godmother had to write up the paperwork. On the serviette it stated that 'I, Emily Brooks, will never marry and never have children.' I read it over in the bubble bath with the pen in my hand, and signed on the dotted line. *Good*, I thought. *Now she will take me seriously.*

I am no longer five but things have not changed for me. I do not have the serviette—it is in the equivalent of my godmother's shed somewhere and she has been trying to locate it—but that does not matter. Because ever since that bubble bath, that signature has been seared in my mind, and it is the one thing I always seem to own. While I am a recovering chronic adapter, this is the one thing I don't appear to adapt. A lot of people find it funny, or offensive, or selfish, or odd. But I don't mind. They do.

I tell you this story not so you can form some opinion of me being funny or offensive or selfish or odd. I tell you this story because it is mine to own. And throughout my time owning this story I have been greeted with the surprised faces of many men. Most are shocked when I tell them I do not want to marry or have children. I apparently look like the type who would. And they all want to marry and have children. But of course they do, because they have never really had to deal with much of a trade-off. Women, on the other hand, have and do and I'm not sure if I want to deal with the trade-off. I'm not sure about marriage and kids at all. I might change my mind. I am told I will, by both men and women. But at the moment, I have not changed it. So, I tell men about that serviette and the bubble bath, so they know who I am and what I want and maybe most importantly, what I do not want. I want a great love and a teammate to walk through life with, but that is about the extent of it.

It is important to talk about what you do not want. It is equally important to talk about what you want. I am talking, of course, about the little piece of earth you hope to claim. This little piece of earth encompasses your values and dreams and ambitions and equates to the life you want to lead. Whether that is with a family or without one, moving overseas or staying put, becoming the next prime minister or moving to the Byron Hinterland to start your own kombucha brand, it is crucial to own this, and claim this, because it drives the direction of your story. And if you do not own it, it becomes rudderless, and susceptible to the currents of every romantic encounter.

Owning your story and continuing to claim your little piece of earth does the opposite. It helps you maintain who you are and what you want in every romantic encounter, while also filtering out the incompatible from the compatible: the men who want completely different things to you from the men who want similar things to you. Relationships, like life, are shades of grey, so some level of compromise is always required at some point along the way, but shrinking yourself along the way never is. In fact, it is not only *not necessary* in relationships, it is *not good* for relationships. Shrinking yourself and not claiming your little piece of earth prevents Teammate Love from showing up in your life.

Stephanie Coontz agrees that women still often shrink themselves and their desires, and it doesn't do us any good. 'There's one thing I've learned from scores of oral histories,' Coontz told me. 'Women's socialisation to protect people's feelings and to ruminate about things leads to a tendency to hint at what we want or just hope our partner will get it.' When we are not up front about what we want, we let things simmer until we can tolerate it no longer. 'At that point,' continued Coontz, 'we raise our disappointment in sharp, critical ways that trigger men's socialisation to be especially reactive to feeling disrespected. And that is a problem.' Essentially, we need to talk about what we want within our relationship before the small problems become big problems.

If you shrink yourself and deny your ambition and enter a relationship under a false pretense, you will likely lose the little piece of earth you were hoping to claim.

This is worse than The Cool Girl because you are not just being deceptive about who you are, but what you want, and therefore the man you will share your future with— however long or short—cannot support what you want, because he is not aware of the full extent of it. You have hidden it, so he has no chance.

If you end up staying with this man, when it comes to starting a family he will assume your little piece of earth is not as important as his, and therefore his ambitions, his career and his desires come first. And you cannot lose your shit over this, because you indirectly told him his little piece of earth had priority by not owning yours. More often than not, you will reach a place—just like The Cool Girl eventually does, just like Nicole in *Marriage Story* did—where you *will* lose your shit over this. You will probably have a house and half a career and two-and-a-half children and it will be messy. All because you didn't front up at the start and talk about what you want, out of fear he would not find it desirable. Only to arrive at a destination that is definitely not desirable, because do you know what is not working now? Your relationship, and probably, your life, because you have shrunk yourself so much that you don't know who you are anymore. It is far better to own your story and claim your little piece of earth at the start. It does the work for you. (More on how to claim your little piece of earth in Chapter 12.)

A Teammate Will Listen

As owning our stories and claiming our little pieces of earth are now the solutions, they will remove from the romantic equation the men who don't admire and respect women with whole lives. The good news being that the men left in the equation love women owning their own lives. So, they have the chance to love you! And the love these men will deliver will be Teammate Love, because they know where that ambition and independence and self-ownership leads you, just like Marty did with Ruth. It leads you toward a piece of earth just as important as theirs. So, they will share the load, but most importantly they will be willing to share the load because they signed up for it. That may be the best part of the process: all you have to do is show up and tell your story, and along the way continue to claim your little piece of earth. There is no maneuvering, no games, no deception. If you arrive at every date not only being yourself but being open about what you want and listening to what he wants, you are setting up an honest foundation for a future relationship and solid partnership.

Now, obviously you need to take social cues into account. It's not so much a matter of saying on date one, 'I want to have three babies by thirty, and I want to be married before then, and that is only seven years away so we better move quickly on this,' or, 'I want to be the

Prime Minister by forty-five. Are you ready to be a First Husband?' It is a matter of not hiding what you want or talking it down or shrinking yourself to make him feel more comfortable. Because that is not going to result in happiness for either of you. By being open, you find the Teammate Love worthy of you and right for you.

Talking down your story hands over your power, and the man before you will eventually own your story. Soon enough, you lose control of it and you've moved into *his* apartment with *his* furniture and you never develop your own taste just like Nicole, and this is probably just the beginning. Your life only becomes smaller while his expands. That is not his fault either, because he is only seeing what he wanted to see and shaping this relationship around what he wants. Men have been owning their stories for centuries, and he is no doubt owning his while you are not owning yours. So, make him see your story by owning it. It doesn't mean your story can't change or grow. It is your story to change and grow with. I may end up proving that serviette wrong and have two-and-a-half children with my teammate of a husband and my mother will roll her eyes for eternity. The point is that it is my story to write, it is my little piece of earth to claim, not anyone else's. And along the way, why wouldn't I own it? It's mine.

Chapter 7

Put the U Back in Beauty

I have a friend who is the type of woman who could talk herself into Rihanna's birthday party and dance on stage to Diplo's DJ set at a three-day music festival. Actually, she's not the type of woman who could do that—she has done that. That shit just happens to her, while the most exciting part of my day is usually having my morning coffee made by someone else.

My friend is beautiful. In fact, she is a model. She has big hips and big thighs that are photographed in fashion shoots and featured in beauty campaigns. But I don't think it's her beauty that drags her into these ridiculous situations. Or her big thighs. Her curves have not always been popular, yet she loved them well before body positivity came along. And it is *this* trait that gets her into these extraordinary situations. Her ability to love and have confidence in herself, no matter what, gives off a certain charm. And people always want a part of it.

I am talking about my friend, Jessica Vander Leahy, here because this is a chapter about beauty in a book

about love; and we cannot examine women's relationship with love properly without examining our relationship
with our physical appearance. Jessica Vander Leahy has a
positive relationship with hers, which most women do not.
And it's important to listen to the positive stories, to learn
and grow and eventually reconcile our own.

To be a young woman is to slowly realise where much
of the world sees your value: in your beauty. You might
first revel in it, then focus on it, then fight it, and eventually let go of it entirely. If you don't, this beauty that society
links with youth will eventually disappear whether you
want it to or not. The reason women have such a complex
relationship with our physical appearance—our beauty—
is because society has always told us that this is where
our power lies.

We are informed about this from childhood. I grew up
with adults telling my parents what 'beautiful girls' they
had. 'Beautiful' being the adjective that always came first.
I was blue-eyed, blonde-haired and slender. I held all the
social capital a young girl needed to get ahead in this world
and feel good about herself. Yet I didn't. I don't think many
of us do. Because all those comments did was reinforce the
necessity and importance in being 'beautiful', and when
those comments didn't appear in a social interaction I felt
like I was doing something wrong. You become invisible
and ordinary, so you strive harder to become beautiful

again. If you do, society will offer up the reward: attention, praise, power.

Women's beauty was historically—and fancifully—associated with perceived high levels of fertility, which is why it is so intertwined with youth. So, strong men fought for beautiful women, and today many men still do. A woman's attractiveness is still one of the most important factors for men when choosing a romantic partner.

In his 1972 book *Ways Of Seeing*, art critic John Berger accurately wrote: 'Men look at women. Women watch themselves being looked at.' He argued that women learn from childhood to continually survey themselves, growing up to never exist without the shadow of the male gaze. 'This determines not only most relations between men and women but also the relation of women to themselves . . . she turns herself into an object—and most particularly an object of vision: a sight.'

When I read this statement it resonated on such a cellular level that I felt like I had fallen deeper into myself, suddenly knowing that person I walked around with a little better. I started to notice how quickly I would pick up on men's glances, and I also saw it in the women around me. We are always watching ourselves, and examining how the world interacts with our physical presence.

It is this relentless examination that is so insidious to our lives because it constantly feeds the narrative that this is where our worth lies. So, we channel our energy and focus into an unreliable investment. Only to wait for our wrinkles to arrive, and the heads to turn less and less often. As Gloria Steinem once said, 'We're made to feel that our bodies are ornaments, not instruments.'

Seeing the Instrumental, not the Ornamental

There is a reason Jessica Vander Leahy has an unwavering appreciation for her body and herself. She was born in Papua New Guinea, where women's bodies were viewed and treated differently than in the West. 'Bodies were seen as functional,' she told me, as we sat on my grey couch with mugs of tea in hand. She recalled a famous photograph from the area she was raised in. In it, a woman breastfeeds her child on one breast and a pig on the other. Pigs represented wealth, and the status of your family was judged by the number of pigs you owned. You had to keep a child alive, but you also had to keep your pigs alive. The photograph didn't sexualise or objectify the woman's half-naked body. It merely represented both wealth and function. 'It wasn't really ever discussed that your body should be any different [than functional],' she said.

Many people in her community were also battling illnesses and disabilities—the ongoing effects of polio were still present—so when she looked around, all Vander Leahy felt was an 'enormous amount of gratitude' that her body worked. If her surroundings hadn't drilled it into her, her parents made sure they did, and this outlook stayed with her as she moved to the West, where women were told a different story.

When she arrived in Australia later in her childhood, Vander Leahy walked into school and suddenly noticed that her body was 'a lot bigger' than those of the other girls. It was an acute observation more than an internal critique; the roots of her childhood unwavering.

'My genetics are made to climb up mountains, so I have this big arse and big calves and strong thighs, but I remember seeing these girls with very twiggy legs and thinking, "Oh, my legs are so much bigger,"' she said. 'There is nothing wrong with observing your body as different and having [an] appreciation for it. I played a lot of sport, so my body was always seen as something pretty powerful in my mind.'

Vander Leahy views her body somewhat like a man does: instrumental, not ornamental. And for women like me, who have been told the alternative story, the answer to reconciling our relationship with our physical appearance lies in choosing this viewpoint: in seeing our body and face as instruments that allow us to swim and run and sit and stretch and smile. Instruments that carry our mind and personality around so that we can think and converse and laugh and use these assets to form relationships.

In order to do this, we must first shift our perspective and instead of seeing the flaws in our bodies, choose to see the function. Once you see the function, you can feel gratitude for what you have, just like Vander Leahy. You begin to focus on what you *do* have, instead of what you don't. But it does not end here.

This perspective still leaves us focusing on our bodies, so it helps to make this world smaller and the other, bigger. When we channel our focus and energies toward our minds and our interests and our personalities and our intrinsic lives, the weight of our external beauty becomes lighter; its world, smaller. Our worth is defined less by it, as our internal world takes the front seat in our value and our lives.

We have to consciously invest in these other facets of ourselves more than men do, because we have been conditioned to focus on the external more than men have. It is traditional for men to wield power through their work; it is traditional for women to wield it through their beauty.

The woman of today may no longer need to use her beauty to form a relationship with a powerful man, consequently giving her access to this power. Today she can acquire power (a job, a home, wealth) independently, and choose her relationship on the basis of anything else. Yet she is still made to feel that her beauty is not just important, but crucial to her existence. So, she spends thousands of dollars and hundreds of hours on maintaining a slender, tight physique and clear, poreless skin. Her mind is not just consumed with work each day, but whether her diet is clean enough and her skin bright enough as she mentally beats herself up for eating pasta last night. She strives for this ideal version of her physical self, only stopping momentarily to beat herself up for falling off course.

This all-consuming feeling is one we have to work harder against, in order to live in a world where our bodies are instrumental. Because it is the ornamental aspect that has been used to oppress us time and time again.

The Beauty Myth

In her 1990 bestseller *The Beauty Myth*, author and journalist Naomi Wolf wrote about an unusual trend that saw beauty requirements for women increase as women gained more social power. The second wave of feminism in the 1960s and 70s may have seen their economic and legal dependence on men decrease, but they were now held to stricter physical standards in the workforce. It was like a social reflex stepping in to hold women back from achieving gender equality.

Before the second wave of feminism, women were confined to the home and their worth was attached to the keeping of it. Women's magazines advertised cleaning products, and housewives purchased them with great enthusiasm. After many women freed themselves from the home, the magazine ads continued, only now they were replaced with ads for beauty products—the personal worth women had associated with their home had merely been redistributed onto their appearance.

The 'beauty myth' told women that beauty could be achieved not through pure luck and genetics but through hard work. With enough patting and prodding and purchasing and dieting, they could achieve the beauty they were striving for. And if women did work and did succeed in the workforce, the beauty myth told them that their beauty became even *more* crucial to maintaining this professional success. Being beautiful became an additional part of their job, and if they did not maintain it, they were deemed replaceable. As a result, many women became distracted by anxieties over their appearance instead of focusing on gaining more political and professional power.

Wolf wrote that women of the time had access to more power and independent money than ever, 'but in terms of how we feel about ourselves physically, we may actually be worse off than our unliberated grandmothers'. I don't think the woman of today feels all that different. She still spends thousands of dollars each year on boutique gym classes, purchases expensive serums under the guise of self-care, and rubs a jade roller on her face in the hope of avoiding the effects of gravity.

The beauty myth was so detrimental to women's lives because it behaved as the final system maintaining male dominance, by 'assigning value to women in a vertical hierarchy according to a culturally imposed physical standard', wrote Wolf. Women could be ranked against one another at face value. But the most crucial point here is that beauty is defined by a culture that is ever changing, and therefore the definition of 'beautiful' will always change with it.

You see, we don't get to decide what 'beautiful' is. It is defined by culture, which has been predominantly controlled by men and is constantly changing. While Kate Moss may have been the cultural pin-up of the nineties, it is Kim Kardashian West today. Skeletally thin has been replaced by curves in all the right places and contoured faces, and it is hard for a single woman with a single body to keep up and succeed at every one of these ideals.

This evolving nature of beauty drives us to chase it much like the toy rabbit lures the greyhounds around the race track. And the perception that we can achieve it through hard work (be it expensive serums or boutique gym classes) keeps our pace up. Yet if we do already have it or acquire it, its link to female youth means it will inevitably fade over time. If it gives us power, it is only ever for a while.

Play the Hand You're Dealt, and Invest in Your Blue-Chip Stocks

It is important to keep this unreliable nature of beauty front of mind when we slip back into an ornamental mind-set over instrumental. We cannot ever be comfortable in life and in our relationships if we assign our value and worth to our physical appearance.

Beauty *is* largely based on pure luck and genetics. We can make ourselves look a little different with hard work, but we cannot change ourselves entirely. And in the end we grow old, and as beauty is largely linked to youth, we become less conventionally beautiful over time. 'If you're going to be a smart girl about being beautiful, you've got to know that your beauty is not a blue-chip stock,' Vander Leahy said. 'So, invest in your blue-chip stocks.'

We are all dealt a different hand in life, but what is important is how we play those cards. Beauty is a gift, but so is our sense of humour, our personality, our charisma, our intelligence. The greatest gift we can give ourselves, though, is our choices in this life. We decide what we invest in. We choose how we spend our time and navigate our lives.

As a young woman it is important to understand that the history we have inherited will influence how we make those choices. Being told I was a 'beautiful girl' only maintained my focus on it. The diets began in my late teens and remained until I was about twenty-two, when I realised my days were stacked against calories and my notebooks had become food diaries. Now I wonder what I could have done with that time? That energy? That focus?

I don't think my relationship with food and weight and appearance has been any more complex than that of the average woman, but after a while you begin to wonder why you're chasing it so hard. That ideal woman you see is never really within reach. I don't diet anymore and now I feel better about my body than I did during those years, because my days are consumed by my internal life more than my external. It doesn't mean I don't care about my external appearance, but it makes up a smaller sum of my worth.

I still see the attention, praise and power that comes with being thin. Men take more notice of you and women want to know how you've done it; for women, that reaction is often louder than when we announce we've just received a promotion. But you can take notice of these things without buying in. In fact, noticing it helps you stop buying in as enthusiastically.

We can decide our way into an existence that will grow with us, over an unreliable one that will only fade. 'The relationships that you value aren't ones that are based on the way you look, because that is absolutely guaranteed to change. You will 1000 per cent look like a completely different person [as you age]. It's not a viable foundation to base a relationship on,' said Vander Leahy.

Finding a Love That Grows With You

By channelling our energy into the other facets of ourselves, we change our position in romance. If we see our value outside of our physical appearance, we're more likely to align ourselves with someone who sees the same value in us that we see in ourselves. This is a value that will increase over time, instead of deplete as we age, and we therefore can live in a love that will grow as it continues to see more worth and value in us each year.

We can't change all men by changing our behaviour, but if you value your sense of humour and intelligence, you are not going to choose to be with someone who only values your exterior. When your values shift, your compatibility shifts. Take compliments as an example.

If you focus heavily on your appearance, you will value the romantic partners who compliment your appearance more than anything else. If you value your intrinsic confidence, you will value the romantic partners who compliment that attribute more heavily.

Vander Leahy recalled a recent trend she has noticed in her love life, where men have been saying more regularly, 'I love your confidence.' It is these men with whom we need to form relationships. The men who see and appreciate our intrinsic value—they are the men who will offer up Teammate Love. Because this is a love based on something so much deeper than our exterior. It isn't something that can be judged at face value and placed in a vertical hierarchy. It isn't comparable.

The make-up of your intrinsic life, your selfhood, is something unique to you. The men who offer only praise for your exterior—well, you know the type of men they are. They will likely judge on face value, compare women to other women, and place you in a vertical hierarchy, which is not a reassuring relationship to live in. Your values choose the path you wander.

It is hard to not value our appearance. Particularly when our lives are performed on Instagram in return for daily metrics that decide how good our lives are depending on the images we share; when online dating leaves us reduced to, and selected by, an image. But as Vander Leahy told me, 'It doesn't make you instantly interesting just because you're beautiful. It can get someone's attention and that's about it. And that should be about it.'

It's important to continue investing in the parts of ourselves that are interesting and will grow more interesting over time because they do not just define who we end up with, they influence how happy we are in our relationships down the track. As Jim Harrison wrote in *The Road Home*, 'The days are stacked against what we think we are.' And if you live in a world and a relationship where your days are stacked against your physical appearance, you live in a reality built on fear and comparison and unreliability. If, however, you live in a world where your body is seen as a loveable instrument that carries around everything that makes you, you, your days are stacked against confidence and comfort. It is also a world that is so much more fun.

Whenever I find myself falling out of this world, I repeat a quote I stumbled upon while watching Netflix's *John Mulaney & the Sack Lunch Bunch*. At the end of the children's comedy show, when all the children state their existential fears and anxieties (which, if you were wondering, are the same as our adult existential fears and anxieties), performer André De Shields says: 'There *is* no one like you. There *has never been* anyone like you. There *will never be* anyone like you. Therefore, be yourself.'

It always allows me to reenter the world in which Vander Leahy dances. To claim who I am a little harder. To take yesterday's flaws and turn them into today's privileges, because how fortunate we are to be someone no one else is, or has been, or ever will be. We are doing the world a disservice if we hide our individuality in favour of a culturally constructed beauty ideal designed to make us all look the same and behave the same.

Try to see your body as the instrument that carries around your personality and mind, which allow you to form relationships with the people who love you for exactly these traits. Relationships in which you can laugh and converse in and grow with over time, to reach a point where you don't even see the other person physically anymore. My mother once said that. Eventually you reach a point where your partner opens the door and walks back into the house each night, and all you see is your love for them. A love that is like no other, never has been like any other, and never will be like any other. And that sight is one of enormous beauty.

'Beauty is in the eye of the beholder. It's so clichéd but it's so true,' said Vander Leahy. 'As women especially we need to understand that we bring more to the table than just what we look like, and it's important to show that we're creative or smart and have a personality and we have thoughts and feelings behind just the colour of our eyes or whatever it is that gets us noticed.'

If we want to shift the way the world values women, we must first shift the way we value ourselves. Decide what your days look like, and create a world that grows with you, rather than one that fades over time.

Chapter 8

Your Checklist Isn't Your Checklist

A psychologist and economist walk into a bar. They are both professors at different universities. The economist orders two beers, leans over to the psychologist and asks, 'Where is this joke going?'

'Nowhere,' replies the psychologist. 'We are professors. This is a study.'

Ah, yes. The study. These two professors, Sheena Iyengar and Raymond Fisman, are running a series of speed-dating events as part of their study into humans' dating habits and choices. At a humble bar across the road from Columbia University in New York City, eager men and women seeking modern love fill the room. Before the speed dating begins, though, participants are required to fill in a questionnaire that asks what traits they desire in an ideal partner. Categories include 'intelligence', 'attractiveness', 'shared interests', 'sincerity' and 'a sense of humour'. Speed daters fill this out immediately before the dates, immediately after the dates, one month later and again six months later. These questionnaires then become data for

Iyengar and Fisman to analyse how humans choose their life partners.

But, back to the bar.

On this particular evening, author and journalist Malcolm Gladwell was a bystander quietly observing the speed dates being carried out. In his book *Blink,* Gladwell describes how he noticed a woman, whom he named Mary, light up when a man, whom he named John, sat down in front of her. The two locked eyes; Mary leaned toward John, looking down shyly and a bit nervously. To Gladwell, the two showed all the signs of instant attraction. Mary was blonde and pale. John was tall and green-eyed and fit all of the categories Mary ticked in her questionnaire moments before. *Really?* No. Of course he did not. Mary, like the majority of speed daters in the study, could not predict to whom she would be attracted before she sat down. What Iyengar and Fisman discovered was that who people *want* and who people *are attracted to* are, more often than not, completely different people. And something fascinating happens when people meet someone they are attracted to. The study showed that immediately after meeting someone they connected with, most people changed their answers in the questionnaire to match the traits of that person. So, if Mary valued 'attractive' and 'sincere', but then met John who was 'intelligent' and 'funny', she would immediately change her answers to 'intelligent' and 'funny'.

But then something even more intriguing happened. One month later, Mary revisited the questionnaire and answered 'attractive' and 'sincere' again. She, and the majority of people in the study, reverted back to their original checklist. As Gladwell explains, Mary's first description was what she *thought* she wanted. But what she couldn't anticipate was how she'd respond in the first moment of actually meeting someone.

In short, *who we think we want* and *who we actually want* are completely different people. We do not know ourselves as well as we think we do. We cannot predict whom we will connect with, and all too often we don't learn from our previous connections. We revert back to our original conscious ideal, which I like to call our checklist, and we stubbornly stick to it.

The Origins of Your Checklist

Your checklist is essentially a compilation of your answers to the questionnaire *before* you go on a date. However, it is not filled out moments before. It is filled out years before, at around the tender age of seven. It is reinforced by romantic comedies and women's magazines and your mother and maybe your grandmother, and therefore drilled into your consciousness by the time you create a Bumble account. The physical manifestation of your checklist might be a tall, dark, handsome man in a very decent suit, with a very full bank account who can definitely look after you, even though you don't *need* him to, but it's nice to know *he can*. He is successful and intelligent and wealthy. He is the man you imagine bringing home to the Cheshire Cat-sized grin of your mother.

If you're anything like Mary, you date with your checklist in mind. You probably stumble across men you have an instant connection with, and you may entertain the idea of them for a while, but after figuring out they don't have the right career or pay packet or fail in some other irrational checklist item, you let them go. And you continue the search for Mr Checklist, who is probably ghosting you or breadcrumbing you or ignoring you at some party while staring at his checklist on the opposite side of the room as she drinks spicy margaritas with John. How do I know all this? Because I have a checklist too.

The problem with our checklists is they are inaccurate most of the time. You spend your time and energy chasing an ideal you created at seven, and you wake years later to find yourself with, well, two options. Either you wake up to find no one beside you, because you were busy focusing on some apparition of a teammate who probably isn't good for you anyway, and therefore not a teammate. Or, worse, you wake up beside Mr Checklist to find he is no good for you. In fact, Mr Checklist is probably terrible for you because checklists are built on traditional gendered stereotypes—and biases—which Mr Checklist fulfils in spades. The impending relationship with Mr Checklist is, therefore, likely built on the opposite of the Teammate Love you are aspiring to find.

The Problem with Our Checklists

The Iyengar–Fisman speed-dating study not only revealed that women and men cannot predict to whom they will be attracted; it showed what men and women place the greatest weight on when searching for their romantic partner. In essence, men's and women's checklists.

Men place the greatest weight on physical attractiveness, and—as we've already learned—do not always value women's intelligence or ambition when it exceeds their own. Women, on the other hand, value intelligence and race the most highly, while also showing a preference for men who grew up in affluent neighbourhoods. This is essentially our checklist and his checklist, which is not based on mutual professional respect and love, but one party's attractiveness, and another party's proximity to wealth.

When I spoke to Michael Flood about our checklists, he said there is a consistent claim in evolutionary psychology that men and women's traditional partner preferences are 'innate' and 'reflect evolution and biological imperatives'. However, he argued that social and cultural environments actually wield more influence on our checklists. 'They reflect, above all, the influence of gender inequality.' Consequently, the men our checklists choose are going to fulfill roles perpetuating gender inequality. If you choose a man solely because of his wealth, his wealth will remain a priority in your relationship. Down the track, maybe his career is prioritised over yours, and when children come into the picture he maintains full-time work while your career takes the backseat and you work part-time or not at all. Over the years, you bear the burden of unpaid work and caretaking, lose the fulfillment you gained in a career you loved, retire with half the average man's super—the current statistic in Australia—and then who maintains independence and power in the relationship? Probably not you. Consequently, if a man chooses you solely because of your physical attractiveness, as you age, the factor defining your power in the relationship begins to fade and you walk the uneasy road of the shortcut (see page 64).

The result of both men's and women's checklists favours men and handicaps women, because they are influenced by gender inequality—which hands men privilege and women disadvantage. This isn't to say all affluent men and beautiful women are destined for a love less than

Teammate Love, but if they are chosen by their romantic partner solely for these traits, it's not likely to eventuate into a love based on mutual professional respect. It's likely to be based on a power imbalance designed by the gender inequities of the time our checklists were created. They are designed to give him the one-up.

Redesigning Our Checklists for the Better

If the gender inequities of society created our checklists, this also means our checklists can be changed by evolving societies and cultures—and by increasing gender equality. In other words, this means we have the collective power to change our checklists. In fact, evidence shows we are already on our way.

Longitudinal studies show that the gap in men's and women's preferences is closing with increasing gender equality. In more gender-equal societies, the gap in men's and women's partner preferences is far smaller, showing similar preferences in terms of age, income and the qualities they value. Flood used Finland and Turkey as examples, with Finland having much greater gender equality than Turkey. The age gap between partners in heterosexual relationships is much greater in Turkey than in Finland, as is the difference in partner preferences.

'So, in a society where women don't have much economic power, don't have much access to income or education, they're more likely to value a partner who can provide that for them,' Flood told me. While in countries like Australia, the United Kingdom and the United States, where women have greater access to income and education, our priorities are beginning to change. The provider qualities of men become less important and traits such as 'attractiveness' and 'intimacy' become more so. 'Men's and women's partner preferences are shaped by gender roles and gender equalities, and so you see that among men, you see that among women, you see that across society, you see that over time.'

So, while society is on its way to changing our checklists for the better, you can speed up the process by doing the work to actively change yours. We can't berate men for their gendered biases in romance, and not do anything about our own. We should actively work to remove our prejudices, and that can only begin by first being aware of them. Check yourself and your biases every time you stumble across a possible suitor. Don't write off a man at the first meeting because he doesn't have the job title you appreciate or the pay packet you approve of, because it's not only inefficient, rude and judgemental—it's hypocritical. You can't criticise men for devaluing your success, and then only date those coming from a small dynasty or with an MBA from Harvard. Women, just like men, have their own inherent gendered biases based on our socialisation and outdated cultural norms and we must work to change them for both the good men out there and, of course, for ourselves.

Use, instead, meaningful connection and Teammate Love as your navigators. Do you feel a meaningful connection with him? Can he deliver Teammate Love? The answer to the last question takes time, but that is what the rest of this book is for. And if you're struggling to reframe your checklist, remember this: When it comes to big life decisions, would you take advice from a seven-year-old? No. I probably wouldn't even rely on a seven-year-old's advice for small life decisions. The only advice I would take from a seven-year-old is their choice in bedtime reading, so I can enjoy Thai takeout and three episodes of *Law and Order* before their parents arrive home.

Babysitting skills aside, by sticking to your checklist you are not only allowing your life to be guided by the gendered biases you are asking men to remove from their lives, but you are also taking dating advice from a seven-year-old who doesn't exist anymore. On top of all this, it is advice that is also incorrect most of the time. As those professors proved pages ago, we don't always have a spark with Mr Checklist, but the spark never fails with the men with whom we connect. Trying to dictate who you will end up with is not only counterproductive, but results in you missing some great opportunities, great conversations and great men. Time to let go, and see what you stumble upon. Likely, all of the above.

Chapter 9

Stop Looking for Him Instead of Yourself

I have a debatably creepy fascination with older women. While most women are in search of the secret to youth, I am in search of the secret to old age—and these older women appear to have the answer. I use the word 'appear' here because I never actually talk to them. I usually just stare, from afar, and quietly try to work it out by myself. This is where the debatably creepy part comes in.

One of those moments was in the small town of Canggu on the popular Indonesian island of Bali. I was having a coffee this Tuesday afternoon at The Slow, a boutique hotel, and a woman walked in with someone I assumed was her daughter, around thirty, because this woman was around sixty. Or maybe they were friends. That is not the point. The point is she stopped me in my tracks that day, and it wasn't her beauty that did it. It never is. It was the way she held herself. She walked in with her shoulders pulled back, her head held high, and it wasn't arrogance. It was an ease. She knew who she was, and she dressed like it too. Her ripped white denim cut-offs hung low on her hips. The bottom of her singlet of the same tone tied neatly in a knot, exposing a strip of her stomach. Her shorts were held up by a red satin scarf, tied with the cool care of a woman in her sixties who had the balls to wear clear aviator Ray-Bans for every reason other than optical. She had the secret, and I wanted it. But you know how this story goes. I never asked.

There is a beauty to knowing oneself. It is not conventional, not obvious in photos. It is a radiance, clear in person. I don't think it is beautiful because it's easy, but rather because it's hard. There are no shortcuts. It takes time, and patience, and work. But when you arrive at this destination, I have no doubt, it is worth it.

There is a reason older women tend to have this radiance. They have had the time. They have fostered the patience. They have done the work. And what they now exhibit, I believe, is self-worth. And that self-worth allows them to have an ease. To *just be*. They don't compare. They don't compete. They *just are*. There's a popular sentiment floating around on Instagram claiming that 'the freedom of aging as a woman is the ability to just fucking care less', but as Jennifer Aniston said in a recent *New York Times* profile, the freedom doesn't come from aging itself—it comes from having had the time to have done the work. It comes from experience.

Self-worth is something Joan Didion discussed in her seminal essay for *Vogue* in 1961. The essay was not about self-worth, rather it explored self-respect, insightfully honing in on how the two are inextricably linked: 'To have that sense of one's intrinsic worth which constitutes self-respect is potentially to have everything: the ability to discriminate, to love and to remain indifferent. To lack it is to be locked within oneself, paradoxically incapable of either love or indifference.'

And that is why we are here, in a chapter about self-worth in a book belonging to modern love. Because they are inextricably linked. You cannot exist with an ease in love without the presence of self-worth, and often during the search for self-worth, you seek out the external validation of men to fill a void. But this validation, this love, while it is lovely, will never equate to or make up for the presence of your intrinsic worth. And if you are currently filling your life with the romantic attention of men to avoid paying attention to what your heart is truly trying to grasp—a love within oneself—you are seeking out, and probably finding, what I like to call Bandaid Boyfriends. And these men, while possibly great men, will never quite measure up. The answer, the reconciliation, is only ever found within yourself.

Oprah knows this.

Oprah Winfrey was born in Mississippi to a mother and father who promptly split, leaving her with her maternal grandmother on the farm. At six, she was sent to her mother in Milwaukee and later passed on to her father in Nashville. Then back to her mother, then back to her father. A childhood of parental handballing. She had not grown up with love, so instead of giving it to herself, she sought external validation by becoming an 'achiever' and later, in her twenties, she based her worth on the love of men, which she wrote about in her book *What I Know For Sure*. Without a man, she thought she amounted to nothing. It wasn't until years later that she discovered that the deep love and approval she was chasing could only be found within herself. 'What I know for sure is that a lack of intimacy is not distance from someone else; it is disregard for yourself,' Winfrey wrote. She believes we all need relationships (friendships and the romantic kind) that help sustain our lives for the better but they will never 'shush that voice inside you that has always whispered *You're not worth anything*'. Our family and friends will never convince us of that intrinsic worth we crave. Only we have the answer.

The arrival point of self-worth differs for each one of us, which, I guess, adds to its beauty. It depends entirely on our enthusiasm for it, our willingness to embrace it, our self-awareness, our experiences, and as always, our genetic coding. It is easier for some than for others. I have friends who seem to have known and valued themselves from the moment they exited the womb. But my genetic coding has never favoured me in this pursuit, so I have relied entirely on enthusiasm. Meaning, my interest in my selfhood—the quality that constitutes one's individuality—and its consequential worth has been largely a selfish one.

For me, it can only be arranged in that order. Understanding one's selfhood has always had to come first. Before I can own it, embrace it, work with it, respect it, see worth in it, and eventually, love it. To understand my selfhood, I have always had to do the work. To make the space, to go to the journal, to do the meditation course, to try and fail at yoga seven times over, to read, to write, to sit down with the therapist, to run. And like me, most of you will have to do the work or you have already done it or maybe, like a couple of my friends, you will glide through it. For me, each attempt has been different. Some inch you closer, some pull you further away, and some leave you with a case of mistaken arrival. A moment of clarity appears until, minutes or days later, it is knocked about and eventually lost again. But gradually, through each setback and each breakthrough, you inch your way closer and it quietly appears in your life.

Its arrival for each of us is different, and so our roads to self-worth vary, although the compasses we choose to guide ourselves are of similar ilk. In terms of getting there, I can only write what I know. And what I know is you must first carve out the space to know yourself, to understand yourself, to learn what it means to be you. It begins with space. This space doesn't come with parties or brunches or long walks with girlfriends or dates with men or scrolling on your phone. It is an entirely personal act. It occurs, of course, alone. And just as we schedule in time for the parties and the brunches and the long walks with girlfriends and the dates with fine men, we must book in the dates with ourselves. To learn a little more about the person who appears in front of us in the mirror each morning. To look closely. To listen. Whether that occurs through the journal, or meditation, or the long walk with only yourself as good company, is entirely up to you.

It is when you can hear the little voice inside you that tells you what it means to be you and signals where you want to go. You must make the space for it. You must get quiet. Because this little voice doesn't scream or come with subtitles. It whispers. And when you listen to the whispers you start to understand yourself a little better, know yourself a little more intuitively, and through the simple act of paying attention you do right by yourself more often.

Self-respect, Didion wrote, does not concern matters of reputation or the approval of others but involves 'a separate peace, a private reconciliation'. It begins and ends with: the dates we book in with ourselves. We must continue to give back to ourselves, whether we have found worth there yet or not. It cannot be faked, she wrote, but it can be developed. We can pull forward its arrival in our lives if we are disciplined about it.

Once we know what it means to be us, once we respect ourselves, we can find worth there. While I have always done the work to make the space, the tool that facilitated self-worth's arrival on my doorstep, quietly allowing itself in, was a 2016 *Longform* podcast episode featuring an interview with Heather Havrilesky, an author and the Ask Polly advice columnist for *New York* magazine. In response to the interviewer's final question, 'How do you be a person in the world?', Havrilesky answered, 'You've got to lean way in to what you already are.' 'Lean *way* the fuck in.' She suggested looking at the 'so-called worst' parts of yourself and working out how to celebrate them. For me, this counterintuitive approach made all the difference.

Since hearing that answer, I have leant into the 'worst' parts of myself. I have always disliked my tendencies to be emotional, and vulnerable, and to overthink, but since hearing Havrilesky's words, I have leant way the fuck into them. I have found a way to celebrate them, and through them I have begun to know what it is to be me, and also respect what it means to be me. If I can respect the 'worst' parts of myself, I can respect myself entirely. My worth has been reconciled through the lens of these parts and worked itself backwards from there. And I feel I have arrived at a destination of sorts. It may not be the final destination, but it is somewhere.

Didion wrote that people with self-respect exhibit a certain toughness that was once seen as character, a virtue that had fallen down society's list when she wrote it. Its fall has only escalated in the current age. Character forces us to take responsibility for our lives, she wrote, which is where self-respect always begins.

And once you live in this world, where you take responsibility for yourself and own who you are, where your actions matter, you also live in a world you can control, instead of a world that happens to you. The love you grew up without or never fully knew is a love you have given back to yourself. The next heartbreak you experience is one you can work through. The next relationship you look for isn't one you need. It is not a matter of validation. It is not a bandaid. It is a relationship adding to your life, not filling it. You walk explicitly with a sense of want, not a sense of need. Everything you need, you have already given to yourself or can give to yourself. You don't require someone else to give it to you.

When you have found your own sense of worth, not only will it stop you from being taken advantage of, you will be sought out by a man who values a woman who knows her worth. You will also only seek out men who value women with worth, as opposed to men who prefer to take advantage of women's low self-esteem. Once you stumble upon this good man, it will allow you to be a better teammate because you will not rely on your teammate to bring you happiness.

When discussing the defining traits of a good relationship, my girlfriends and I often return to the words of Will Smith. In an Instagram story, Smith explained that you can make another person smile and laugh, but you cannot make them happy. Their happiness is out of your control, and your happiness is out of theirs. He shared that when he and his wife, Jada Pinkett Smith, wed, they both 'came into this fake romantic concept' that they would become one. Not two. And their individual happiness became a collective responsibility until, one day, he 'retired' from the concept. They decided they would both find 'individual, internal, private, separate joy' and present themselves to the relationship again with full cups, instead of begging the other person to fill theirs. 'It's unfair and it's kind of unrealistic and can be destructive to place the responsibility for your happiness on anybody other than yourself,' Smith said.

This version of love liberates. Both parties are responsible for their happiness. One path does not bulldoze the other, one teammate does not ask the other to leave their path and join theirs. One person does not define the other's path or worth. You both walk your separate paths, together.

I do not know where along this journey to self-worth you are, but if you stumble upon a man and choose to walk your futures together before self-worth arrives for you, that is also okay. As many young women who have fallen in love years before they were ready to can attest, sometimes you find love before your see worth clearly in yourself. There is nothing wrong with this place, but the route forward you take matters, and that comes down to attitude. If you have arrived at a new love with the hope he will fix you, please know, he will not. It is up to you, not him. He can push you in the right direction by showing you that you are worthy of love, and often he will, but he cannot make you *know* that you are worthy of love. It is up to you to make the time. To have the patience. To do the work. And eventually, you will walk your two separate paths, together. You will walk from a place of control, and with that comes a sense of ease. Much like the ease of that woman in the white denim cut-offs and clear aviator Ray-Bans worn for every reason other than optical.

Chapter 10

He's Just Not That Into You, or It's Not About You

In the winter of 2016, I met a man. I knew many men at that point in my life but I didn't like any of them. Well, not in the way you're assuming. I had men who were friends, men who were acquaintances, men who were best friends and they were all great, but I didn't *like* any of them.

Heartbreak stings everyone differently. Some jump straight back into the cool company of lust, and sometimes that leap leads back into love. But that always seemed like whiplash to me. I have always opted for the Steer Clear Method when it comes to heartbreak. A good six months, when it comes to physical contact, another five years when it comes to anything beyond physical contact. That is probably not advice you should follow, and that was my attitude at twenty, so maybe I've changed, but I don't think so. I like to sort the baggage before I step onto the next train.

We are not here to talk about trains, though. We are here to talk about men, and in the winter of 2016 the baggage of my 2011 heartbreak was left on the platform, because I had met a man.

He was new to town and he delivered every item on my checklist. We had the same friends. We went to the same parties. Parties we could now arrive at together. We were similar, but not too similar. Different, but not too different. I was smitten. Everyone who knew us was smitten. And maybe that was why it felt so right. It worked for everyone. *We* were happy. And for the first time in five years I was not only happy—I was ready. It was worth it. I was all in. And so was he.

Until he wasn't.

The problem with heartbreak is that it arrives on the doorsteps of people's lives at different times, and this man was at a different point in his. He was still holding onto baggage, and he didn't want to get onto another train yet. He needed time and space. But what he didn't realise was that he had already stepped onto another train, and that train was me; a train that hadn't fully stopped for another person for half a decade. So, it meant something. It was about two months in, and I was happy. Everyone was. And then he took it all away with a text claiming he was *not ready* and he was *sorry* and I was *amazing* but clearly not amazing enough, or something. There was no real reason at the time, which was the confusing part. He was also really nice about it—aside from the chosen communication method—which was the frustrating part. So, I couldn't argue, and I wouldn't have wanted to anyway, because

I'm not the type of person to push someone into some-thing I know they don't want. So, I respected his wishes. I was done. It was done. Our trains would keep moving.

But that's not the end of this story. It's only the start.

If it had ended there it would have been fine. I probably would have recovered quickly, but we had a problem. The parties we once arrived at separately, and then together, we arrived at separately again. We had to coexist in those parties and it never ended well. Because he would drink and I would drink and he would try again, just for the night, and I would usually cave, to some degree. And then I would get mad. Or I would ruminate on the possibility that *just maybe* he was coming around to the concept of 'us'. The short story is, it was a headfuck.

The much longer story is a complicated one. Because during our short time together, we had booked a holiday with friends in Byron Bay for New Year's Eve. This was in August, and New Year's Eve is obviously in December. You know what happened in between: The Relationship That Never Happened. So, from August to October we fumbled our way through the parties. Until I stopped going. Then December came around, and the day before the road trip to Byron Bay I almost pulled out. But I had paid, and so had my friends, and they needed me. I couldn't let them down. So, I went. And it was fine, until the first night, so it really wasn't fine for long.

The first night, at the pub in Byron Bay, was one of those nights where something was just working. As my girlfriend and I danced, we were giving off a certain vibe and a substantial number of men wanted a part of it. We laughed at one point because it was timed a little too well, but someone—this man—did not think it was well timed. He asked me not to 'put' him 'through this'. And then he chased me all night, until eventually, I gave in again. And the entire trip was a power trip of him giving in and me giving in until it was just accepted by the group that we were *a thing* for the trip, but only for the trip.

When we arrived home, seven days and one headfuck later, this man and his best friend dropped me to my apartment. It was dark, and late. We were all tired. They helped me collect my bags from the boot of the car. I loaded them onto my shoulders and arms, except for the remaining one, which this man was holding. But instead of walking me to the door and taking a moment to step up and say goodbye to something we both knew was nothing but a facade so we could coexist at a very long party, he stood by the car and handed me my bag and . . . nothing. I walked to my door, alone, and went inside, sans closure.

He didn't even have the audacity to pretend he cared. But he did have the audacity to message a few days later in a group message. Some joke, I think. We were mates. But we were not. I was done being mates. I was done.

I didn't reply, and he came back around with a text—sent just to me this time—about dropping off a pair of swimmers I had left in the car. I told him to arrive at a certain time, when I would be home. I would get my closure then, I thought. But a few hours later I received another text saying he'd left my swimmers on my patio.

The hide.

I had nothing to lose at that point, so I called with a demand. He picked me up. We drove around the block a few times to the soundtrack of me telling him he did not get my friendship if he did not want the other part, which he had made very clear he did not want. Enough. And *enough* is the operative word here. He did not want it enough. He did not want me enough. But it took six months of an unnecessary emotional beating for me to realise this. He did not want me enough. Or he did not want me enough to put out his timing.

This may have happened to you. Or to someone you know. Or maybe you have been this person for someone else. Regardless, you know this story. It's one we will all see or experience. Because at some point in our lives we meet someone and it doesn't work. Despite how much we want it or how perfect it seems to be, it is not perfect, because they don't want it enough. For men, I have decided, there are two ways they don't want this enough: he's just not that into you, or it's not about you. Of course

I have graciously stolen the first part from the book of the same name. And it is as simple and complicated as that. Sometimes people just aren't *that* into you, and there is no negotiating around it.

When He's Just Not That Into You

Where women and men become confused here, is the line. Someone can be into you enough to spend every drunken Friday night with you, or be with you when you bump into each other at the next party. But when they're not into you enough to take you on a proper date or follow up the next week or take any reasonable steps to move the relationship forward, they're just not *that* into you. Don't give them the benefit of the doubt. The problem most of us make here is we do, because we don't want to believe we are not enough for this person to take the next step forward. So, you make excuse after excuse for them, or attempt to persuade, or lure, only to wake up six months later to the realisation that nothing has changed. You are still not enough. And you have just spent six more months making excuses in the hope that you are proven wrong and they will step up and finally realise that you are right for them. You are better than that. I was better than that.

When It's Not About You, but Peter Pan

Sometimes, though, we have a different problem. Sometimes they *are* that into you, but not enough to put out their timing. After almost a decade observing women and men in Sydney, I have grown to believe there is a major difference between men and women's behaviours when the roadblock of timing pops up. Generally, women will put out their timing for the right man, whereas men will not do the same for the right woman. For men, it is *all* about timing. They tend to settle for a woman pretty quickly once they are ready. It's not so much about the calibre of the woman. And if they stumble upon the right woman at a time when they are *not* ready, they will often let her go in the name of options. For women, however, it is *all* about the calibre of man—and love. They will wait as long as they need to. And regardless of whether or not they are ready, if the right man comes along, women will generally put their timing out for him.

So, when I stumbled upon the Guttentag-Secord theory, I realised my generalisation actually held some weight. Men and women do behave differently when it comes to committing to love, and it is exacerbated by the number of the opposite sex hanging around. It is exacerbated, I guess, by options. The theory was developed by two psychologists and published in their 1983 book *Too Many Women? The Sex Ratio Question.* This theory claims that a person is less dependent on the opposing gender if they have a greater number of potential alternatives. This gives them a greater 'dyadic power'. To look at it collectively, if, for example, there are more women than men in a city or situation, men have greater 'dyadic power', and the opposite is also true if the genders are swapped. You would think this is a simple trade-off—whoever has more options has the one-up. But unfortunately for women, this is not how it plays out in reality. We are screwed either way.

In societies where men outnumber women, women used their 'dyadic power' to create loving relationships and raise families. Divorce is low and the traditional roles associated with women—the mother and the homemaker—are widely respected. However, in these societies, men use their greater numbers to limit women's political and economic power. Consequently, women's participation in the workforce and female literacy decrease. On the other end of the equation, in societies where women outnumber men, men do not use their 'dyadic power' to form loving relationships. They instead become more promiscuous and less committal. Fewer people marry in these societies, and if they do, they wed later in life. Motherhood and homemaker roles for women are also not valued highly in these societies. And as men capitalise on the greater number of available romantic candidates around them, women channel their ambitions instead toward their educations and careers, which appear more reliable than the men around them. Sound familiar? So, either way, women lose out. We are either held in high regard and have loving relationships but low socioeconomic power, or we have our careers but are dealing with non-committal men.

In 1988, the Guttentag-Secord theory was tested by two sociologists, Scott J South and Katherine Trent. They analysed data from more than 117 countries and discovered that, in most cases, the theory was supported. In countries where there were more men, there were more married women and less divorce but also fewer women in the workforce. Maybe the most fascinating observation they came to was that the Guttentag-Secord dynamics were more extreme in developed countries than developing countries. When you look at the cohort of university students around the western world, women outnumber men in spades. I recently told my girlfriend about the Guttentag-Secord theory and she explained that when she was at university in London, the men who did not look like your classic Casanovas would be dating five different women who *were* complete catches, and the men were still not committing to any one of these women. While she would sit beside these men trying to explain they were batting above their average and should lock down one of these women before their lucky streak disappeared, they would look at her with nonchalance. And you know how this story ends—they didn't listen.

When I found the Guttentag-Secord theory, I felt like I had spent eight years grasping at thin air and had finally been handed the answer. After collecting a small pool of qualitative data from my girlfriends' dating lives and my own, I had grown to believe there was a rise in the non-committal man—which can also be described as men with Peter Pan Syndrome. But these men only really seemed to appear in bigger cities. While the men I knew in country towns and small cities all appeared to settle around the median age of twenty-five, the men I knew in big cities like Sydney would mess around until twenty-five and then keep on going, continuing to enthusiastically prosper in the seemingly endless pool of available women for another decade, when they would wake up one day and think, 'Ah, shit. I need a wife.' They would spend the following six months looking for one, and then *ta-da*: she would arrive.

After I'd spent about two years in Sydney, my mother began asking me about the dating scene here and I would inform her that men were boys until at least the age of thirty-two and there was no point trying to seriously date anyone younger than that. My former boss, who has lived in Sydney for far longer than I, jokes that boys don't become men until they hit forty.

But when we move from the physical world into the virtual world, things become even more interesting. Let's consider now how the Guttentag-Secord theory applies to the realm of online dating. Every time you open a dating app there is an endless offering of the opposite gender available to you, in the palm of your hand. If we apply the Guttentag-Secord theory to it, women will generally use their 'dyadic power' to find love and companionship while men will generally use their 'dyadic power' to fuck around. Most dating apps, I believe, have given the non-committal man a pat on the back, and told him to go out and conquer and breadcrumb and pursue as many women as he pleases for however long he pleases and when he is done, he is able to let them down easily and, maybe most importantly, without consequence. In many cases, he doesn't even have to have a conversation. All it takes is a text, or in some cases, an Instagram photo.

For an example of this delightful behaviour, I present to you a case study portraying the wonderful destination humanity has reached. My girlfriend had been dating a man for six months, give or take. They had spoken almost every day and caught up two to three times a week. She was about to leave town to holiday in Bali with her friends, while he was heading to Europe to visit his.

Just before she left, he almost pulled the pin on his European trip to join her holiday in Bali, but she told him to stick with the plan, and visit his friends in Europe. So, they went their separate ways to holiday, only for my girlfriend to stumble across a photo on Instagram of the man she had been dating for six months holidaying with his 'girlfriend'. He had been untagging himself from his 'girlfriend's' photos so they didn't appear in his Instagram feed; nevertheless, my friend stumbled upon one anyway. Then another. Then another. She ended it and he responded a few months later—yes, you read that correctly—asking whether he could meet her to apologise in person. She told him a time. And as she expected when she replied to his message, she received radio silence. He never responded.

Online dating does not just enable the Peter Pans of the world to fly through romance without ever growing up. It allows Peter to behave like a child without any accountability.

Peter Pan, and the Injustices of the Ticking Clock

The rise in non-committal men is a huge problem that creates a power imbalance—and it is almost impossible for women to solve. It has a serious impact on our ability to settle down, and also to start a family. Not only are the Peter Pans of the world taking longer to commit to women, but they progress the relationship more slowly, delaying marriage and children. At a 2019 event for *Future Women*, fertility specialist Dr Raewyn Teirney spoke about the frank realities of fertility and conception as well as the myths that plague Australia and the western world. She explained that women are increasingly delaying motherhood, the age of having their first child dropping from an average of twenty-five in 1991 to thirty-one today, and that the main reasons—drawn from a Fertility Society of Australia study—include women not having a partner (one in three women in their thirties don't), women wanting to establish their careers and have financial security before becoming a parent, and finally, a lack of awareness among women and men around the roadblocks to conception.

Dr Teirney has worked in the reproductive industry for two-and-a-half decades, training in obstetrics and gynaecology in Sydney before becoming a reproductive endocrinology and infertility specialist, which took her to Cambridge and the Bourn Hall Fertility Clinic, the world's first IVF clinic. As she explained, the Fertility Society of Australia survey showed that a lot of people—including men—simply do not understand the importance a woman's age plays in her ability to fall pregnant. Women, she said, are designed to have children between the ages of twenty and thirty, and our fertility drops from thirty but more drastically from thirty-five onwards. Dr Teirney went on to describe the other big myth surrounding women's fertility: the perception that IVF will easily 'fix' any age problem. As a result, Dr Teirney sees a lot of women in their forties expecting IVF will help them conceive. 'IVF is a great tool,' she said, 'but it cannot fix older eggs ... Men are factories and they produce sperm every day. Mother nature was not kind to women . . . the biggest factor of conceiving is female age.' The issue is not just one for potential mothers. 'Men are not grasping it at all and in fact we should be talking about it in men's magazines . . . Many women want to have a child but their partner says, "Oh, you're too young, I want to be doing this, I want to be doing that." There are so many Peter Pans around . . . That's a huge issue we see all the time in clinical practice is men not committing.'

While I listened to Dr Teirney, I felt an overwhelming wave of rage ensue. As she said, mother nature wasn't kind to women. Our biological clock creates this invisible pressure in our romantic lives to settle down in our thirties, while for men, they can continue to play around until, well, they grow bored of it. Their fertility begins to decline at forty, but they produce sperm consistently while women only have a finite number of eggs, which age much faster. This biological handicap women face hands the power over to men, and we have seen how many of them use it. Men have more time to mess around, so they do. While women will use whatever power they have to find the right person and create love and companionship in their lives. I wish I had an answer to this great biological injustice but I do not have an answer. I do not have a solution. This is, quite simply, a huge injustice women face in love.

The only consolation I hope I can offer you is this. When you meet someone and it doesn't work out because they are just not ready to commit, know that it *really* is not about you. I hope the Guttentag-Secord theory has at least raised your consciousness around the external, systematic and biological factors at play. But it all equates to the same thing, really. Whether he's just not that into you, or it's not about you doesn't really matter. There is nothing you can do, except move on and move forward.

There Is Nothing Wrong with You

There is nothing more comforting than clarity. When I was in the messy middle of The Relationship That Never Happened, I had none. I had a message that said a man didn't want to be with me because he wasn't ready. And a message that said I was amazing. A man who implied the latter at parties while implying the former in the morning. It really did seem to be a case of *it's not about you*, but he was nice, so I wasn't sure whether the timing call was just a polite excuse. So, I began to think it was.

I assumed he just wasn't *that* into me. And with that, I made another assumption: that there was something wrong with me, that I wasn't good enough. This is a dangerous little path to walk down. Timing wasn't the issue. I was the issue. I spent months picking myself apart and working on myself and working out. I thought that would fix it. But of course it would not. Because it was never really about me, so there was no way my behaviour would fix it. It was about us, and something about us was not enough to keep the non-existent relationship moving forward. And that assumption was my mistake.

Whether it was a matter of us lacking compatibility or good timing, none of that was about me. It was not a matter of my worth. So, if you have just come out of a scenario where he was just not *that* into you or it's not about you because it's about timing, know that there is nothing wrong with you. You *are* enough. You are just not right for this relationship with this man right now. I will not tell you not to take it personally, because you will. But I will tell you to work through this feeling with a watchful eye, knowing it is irrational. Use it to work on yourself, as we women do when we come out of relationships, and use it as your power. A power to outgrow it and the feeling of inadequacy. A power to learn from it and move on. Because you will move on. You are meant to, and when you move on, it will be on to something better.

Your Better Is Yet to Come

In the period of trying to work out what was wrong with me, I ended up in a vedic meditation course. I did the course, learned the practice and when my meditation teacher launched a new website, he called. I am a journalist and a writer and he wanted a story on the launch. I was invited to see the website before it launched, and rather than being sent a link I was told to go to an apartment block on a particular street, up a set of stairs, and knock on apartment door four, where my meditation teacher and his developer would be. So, I did.

His developer opened the door, and six months later I ran into this developer again. We went for a coffee, and another. Now when I open my apartment door, he is usually behind it. We have been together for almost four years now. But I would have never met him at that time, when our trains were both ready to stop and pick up another passenger, had I not experienced another heartbreak that made me feel like there was something so wrong with me I ended up in a meditation course. I am grateful

I didn't feel good enough. I am glad to have arrived here. In the end, the worst situation led to the best situation and it is a situation I am not sure I would be in, had I not had the other.

When you move on, one of three things will happen. You will move on and eventually arrive to find another, better man and a better love whose timing is right. Or you will move on and eventually this man who wasn't into you enough (whether it was timing or his attitude) will catch up. Or your life will take a different turn altogether. And it will work. But nothing will work while you wait around. So, take that rejection, sit with it for a while and then suck it up and move on. Because what choice do you have other than to accept what you cannot change? And when you do accept it and move on, what you stumble upon will only be better, no matter who it is with or where you are. And when you arrive into the comforting arms of that next chapter, you will have clarity and you will know it was all worth it. Because you are better for it, and the love you have is better for it because it is Teammate Love—or maybe a greater love with yourself. It is a love that you didn't have to persuade or lure or make excuses for. It is a love that didn't begin with an imbalance of power. It is a love that wants you, now.

Chapter 11

Don't Let Aunty Carol and the Pity Face Get to You

There's a great irony to turning thirty. For women, anyway. You farewell the confusion-filled, mistake-ridden twenties and greet a decade of self-actualisation and contentment. At least, that is how I like to see it. While your twenties are spent mentally wriggling around in yourself, your thirties are when you settle into your very *you*. With that acceptance comes an inner power more conventionally known as confidence. The thirties are magical, or as Maya Angelou describes them, 'a knockout'. For women stepping into their thirties alone, this can be a particularly special period of settling into the most potent version of themselves and their power without compromise.

Until you attend a wedding, and all of a sudden there's a virtual post-it note stuck to your forehead saying, 'Pity Me. I'm Lonely.' Now, you might be lonely—but you might not. You're probably quite fine. You're probably great. But somehow, every time you put on that dress and those heels and maybe a lovely pair of earrings and trundle into a wedding reception, your dinner companions' expressions are all the same. Every goddamn time. It's the Pity Face, and it silently verbalises two things. First, it leans over and whispers, 'I'm so sorry you're still single,' quickly followed by, 'Don't worry, you'll find him,' with an unconvincing wink. And you're like, 'Thank you?'

Then your evening goes one of two ways. You sit through the speeches not listening to one word because your mind has wandered off into a rabbit hole of questions along the lines of why you haven't found someone, and maybe you are repulsive, and yes, you should have just settled for Average Dave in high school. I mean, he still works at the convenience store in your hometown of 2000 people but he would have made a delightful, vanilla husband and father. And he would have scrubbed up pretty nicely in a tux tonight. Yes, Average Dave would be Not So Average Dave in a tux. This rabbit hole takes you further and further down the self-loathing tunnel until you leave the party early with your tail between your legs and a takeaway McDonald's bag in hand before jumping into bed with your reliable companion, a Big Mac.

Or there's the second path, which begins with a defensive, 'It's fine, I'm fine!' and proceeds to you downing seven champagnes during speeches, a solo performance to Trick Daddy on the dance floor, a brief fall, and someone putting you into bed while you scream another muffled, 'I'm fine!' between rounds of vomiting into a bucket. And now you definitely haven't found him because you a) left or b) made a mess of yourself and then left. Good one, honey. But don't worry, you'll find him. *Unconvincing wink.*

But here is the problem. It isn't the seven champagnes, or the Big Mac, or your performance to Trick Daddy. (That was excellent.) It is the way you were made to feel about your singledom. While the Pity Face inherently shows up for single women in their thirties, it doesn't (often) show up for their male counterparts. For men, the presumption isn't, 'They can't find someone.' It is, 'They haven't found someone appropriate to settle down with,' or, 'They aren't ready to settle down.' Men are bachelors with their shiny apartments and cars and annual escapades to Europe, while women are sad spinsters watching Netflix alone with their cat on Saturday night, debating their chocolate's optimal cacao percentage. There is a reason for this. Ironically, the place where the Pity Face most commonly rears its inconvenient head is the foundation on which it was built: the sanctity of marriage. So, before we game the Pity Face, let's remind ourselves why it exists in the first place. Which will, in turn, help you game it.

We have seen that for many generations of women before us, marriage was not a novel pursuit of love, it was a necessity for economic survival. When it came to many avenues of work, finances, property and security, women didn't have the freedom to operate independently, and so it was either walk down the aisle, or live on the street. (Or, if you were fortunate enough, with your parents.) Men, on the other hand, secured a companion, a woman to bear their children and an economic asset in the form of unpaid domestic labour. While the legalities within marriage have evolved to better serve the women who enter them (we now don't lose our credit rating, or our job, and we can keep our last name) the roles of the husband and wife haven't changed dramatically. Women can now work while raising a family, but it means most of us now have two jobs, one unpaid. So, in 2020, why do liberated women in western societies still choose marriage and wifehood willingly?

Ask a woman why she wants to get married and the answer will usually lie in 'tax purposes'. I kid. For many, the answer will lie in 'tradition', and a sense of comfort in having a life partner and a love they can celebrate with those closest to them. Aside from a couple of tax breaks and splitting the cost of living down the middle, the institution of marriage has been romanticised over centuries, and the white dress remains a dream of young girls playing in sandpits. There isn't just *Vogue* and *Cosmopolitan*, there's *Vogue Brides* and *Cosmopolitan Bride*. While women pay witness to cover girls smiling in white gowns, the alternative isn't promoted. Single women pretty much get Carrie Bradshaw. That's it. And while *Sex and the City* marked a great cultural shift for our gender (although, in hindsight, some of it was questionable), reshifting the 'single' perception can't rely on six HBO seasons. Single women are still perceived as lonely and unhappy—their only consolation falling with a large herd of cats—because society has historically told women they required men for economic and psychological security. A husband and children were the missing pieces of the puzzle they needed to find to live out full lives.

In reality, the story we're being sold is outdated and incorrect. The story, today, is very different. The single-and-child-free-by-choice woman is on the rise globally and she couldn't be happier. A 2018 report from the OECD Family Database showed that in almost all OECD countries, marriage rates have declined over the past few decades, with some now half the rate they were. A portion of women are marrying later and conceiving children later but a growing percentage of women are choosing to opt out of marriage and motherhood altogether. They may date, and have relationships, but they are choosing marriage-free, child-free lives.

Social scientist and author Bella DePaulo has dedicated her life's work to shifting people's consciousness around singledom. She is in her sixties, and has been single most of her life. In her TED Talk, 'What no one ever told you about people who are single', DePaulo said she had never heard of embracing singledom, and her work has been dedicated to changing the narrative around it. 'Those [affirming] stories have never been part of our lives the way fairytales have.'

DePaulo pointed to a study around loneliness, depression and stress, where researchers proposed a hierarchy where married women were expected to be the most supported (and therefore least likely to experience loneliness, depression and stress), closely followed by women cohabiting with a romantic partner, then single women who were dating, then single women who were not dating. When they looked at the results, they found little change between the categories. 'The women higher on the hierarchy were not any less lonely, they were not any less depressed, and they weren't any less stressed than the other women,' DePaulo said. 'And the findings for the men weren't that much better.' Marriage or being in a relationship did very little to quell this, despite stories of marriage being celebrated as a union to improve one's life. When couples move in together or marry, DePaulo said, they tend to become more insular, regardless of whether they have children. Single people, on the other hand, are more likely to be involved with their siblings, families and communities, and also have a larger group of friends. 'The story we're told is married people have "the one". The untold, revealing story is that single people have "the ones".' One of the greatest indicators of loneliness for people was if they didn't have a large network of friends to rely on. Friendship was a greater influence than the presence of a romantic partner. 'In the stories we are told, people who live alone are isolated and lonely, but in fact, as long as the people living alone have about the same income as people living with others, they are actually, on the average, less lonely.'

Single women also report higher self-esteem than married women, are having more sex than married women, and again, are more likely to have stronger friendships than their married counterparts. So, while the idea of a single, unmarried woman past the optimal child-rearing age has been built up over decades to be feared or derided, and societal constructs do not consider her path a viable option for happiness, the statistics and the women behind them are proving otherwise. Now, it is a simple case of rebranding. Enter, the Pity Face and a rebuttal in Gloria Steinem.

Giving a New Face to an Established Movement

Feminist activist and writer Gloria Steinem is now eighty-six. While she married eventually, she did not marry until the ripe young age of sixty-six. Today, her iconic long, thick hair has been chopped down to a bob and her clear aviator Ray-Bans are left only in photos of the seventies, reflecting the times and the second wave of feminism in which she became a mother to a generation of women—instead of to her own offspring. To say she has aged gracefully doesn't do her justice. But it never has. Around the time of Steinem's fortieth birthday, a reporter interviewing Steinem offered up a clumsy compliment in that she didn't look forty. 'This is what forty looks like,' Steinem quipped, and recalled later in an interview for *New York* magazine, 'We've been lying for so long, who would know?'

This was, of course, the age society presumed she should be in the trenches of wifehood and motherhood, but in that moment, Gloria Steinem gave a new face to an age in which women felt so disempowered they lied about it. By then she knew the power of speaking her truth. She also knew the power of her appearance and used it as a servant for a greater cause. With it, she changed the perception of a movement and it is a lesson we can apply to our own single lives—and beyond.

As a young freelance writer in 1963, Steinem went undercover as a Playboy Bunny for *Show* magazine, where for eleven days she diarised the horrible working conditions in which Bunnies were forced to operate, from men tweaking their cottontails as they served martinis, to the push-up bras and suffocating waistbands, to the genital examination—which ended following her expose. The piece brought her fame and the first onslaught of attacks over her appearance. It was a piece she regretted writing until she became part of the women's liberation movement. Meanwhile, attacks over her looks continued.

One year later, in 1964, she covered Bobby Kennedy's run for the New York senate. While she shared a cab with Gay Talese and Saul Bellow, Talese reportedly said, 'You know how every year there's a pretty girl who comes to New York and pretends to be a writer? Well, Gloria is this year's pretty girl.'

Four years later, when she joined *New York* magazine as the only female writer on the team, the 'pretty girl' complex still prevailed. 'I was doing politics, but even at the magazine I was still the girl writer,' she recalled years later in a 2015 *New York* magazine profile. As she became interested in the feminist movement, her male colleagues advised her to not get involved with 'those crazy women', and she realised they didn't know who she was because she hadn't actively stated it. She was still considered the pretty girl writer who didn't belong with crazy, ugly feminists. So, she covered an abortion-rights speak-out in Greenwich Village. It was one of the first pieces of mainstream reporting on the women's liberation movement, and from there Steinem realised her writing could be used as activism.

She became a writer, organiser and activist in the women's liberation movement at a time when feminists were popularised as ugly, angry women who couldn't find a husband. But Gloria, all long limbs and thick locks, was the exception. It took someone else highlighting it for Steinem to eventually use it as her power. As Steinem recalled in the same 2015 *New York* magazine profile, she was giving a talk and when her appearance came up, an old woman in the crowd stood up and said, 'It's important for someone who could play the game, and win, to say, "The game isn't worth shit!"' 'I was so grateful to her for understanding that I could use who *I* was to say who *we* were and what *we* represent,' Steinem reflected.

So, how do you raise the consciousness around single women being happy and, in doing so, conquer the Pity Face? You respond to it with a *new* face. Before you crawl down the unproductive rabbit hole of *why no one wants you*, consider *who you didn't want* previously. Consider Average Dave. Would you be happy with Average Dave? Really happy? Down-to-your-very-core happy? You know the answer. Now, that Tinder date last week. Would you be happy with him? No, he wore cargo shorts and had a bong as a coffee-table centrepiece. Now, of course, there was probably the one who got away: Mr Checklist. But as we know he didn't want the real you, so your marriage would have only been a power imbalance most likely fuelled by insecurity. Your previous romantic partners didn't work out because they weren't meant to. Every man came into your life to teach you a lesson about life or your place in it, but they were never meant to remain. Otherwise they would still be here. Tying yourself to one of these men to please society and Aunty Carol doesn't foster happiness.

Knowing that the alternative paths to your singledom wouldn't have walked you into happiness will, I hope, quell some of the questions swirling around in your head and give you more confidence in yourself as a single. Knowing you no longer have to settle for less than Teammate Love in order to find psychological and economic security, like many women before you, also provides a little more. Equip yourself with this knowledge before you enter the next wedding or family reunion, where the Pity Face most often lurks. Also remind yourself that those friendships you have, and the career fulfillment you savour, and the rest of the independent life you have the privilege of enjoying are not shared by all women around the world. It is a great privilege.

And as Aunty Carol's Pity Face shows up while you eat your chicken cordon bleu, you can reply without anger, without defensiveness, without sadness. You can reply with pure contentment and say, 'Aunty Carol, it's fine. It really is. I'm happy.' And then go on to talk about your work, or your friends, or your recent trip to the Amalfi

Coast as she sits there in utter confusion with chicken stuck between her teeth. Show her that this is what single looks like. Show her you could play the game but you're not going to play it with someone incompatible or inadequate or someone who is great but with whom there is simply no spark. You're not going to settle for average. You are looking for Teammate Love, and you're going to be perfectly fine—perfectly happy—in the meantime. Use who *you are* to say who the *modern single woman is.* You can give her a new face, and in doing so slowly remove the Pity Face from our lives.

However, if Aunty Carol still gets under your skin, know this. Focusing on what you *don't* have doesn't help you get what you want. It only harms it. And this is where my good friends Alan Watts and Aldous Huxley arrive in this chapter, because I prefer to lean on philosophers when dishing out advice. Aldous Huxley coined the term 'The Law Of Reversed Effort', which Alan Watts later described as 'The Backwards Law'. These laws, in essence, say the same thing: the more you focus on trying to achieve something, the less likely you are to actually achieve it and the less happy you will be in the process because you are focusing on the *lack of.* Huxley wrote, 'The harder we try with the conscious will to do something, the less we shall succeed.' And in his novel *The Wisdom of Insecurity*, Watts wrote, 'When you try to stay on the surface of the water you sink; but when you try to sink you float . . . insecurity is the result of trying to be secure . . . contrariwise, salvation and sanity consist in the most radical recognition that we have no way of saving ourselves.'

The more you focus on trying to find someone, the more unhappy and afraid and lonely you become in the process, because you're focusing on the *lack of.* The more you try to control a situation, the more you're highlighting the fact you have little control over the outcome in the first place. You're also focusing on what you *don't* have, instead of what you *do.* It leaves you no closer to your desired destination and an unhappier person walking toward it. Being an unhappier version of yourself is not exactly going to help you. So, focus on what you *do* have instead, and let the rest fall into place.

The thing with changing systemic beliefs built upon societal structures and tradition is that you can't just tell people something, you have to show them. You can't tell someone it's fine and then not be fine. You have to show them you're content. And eventually, through the great, consistent work of yourself, your single female peers, a few studies and Gloria Steinem, western society's belief system will eventually change to accept the single woman as happy. But you have to show them the alternative to the angry, lonely cat lady, otherwise they won't believe she exists. You have to Gloria Steinem it.

Chapter 12

Have Your Own Shit, and Keep Doing It

One of my friends and I have a collective dream to one day own an Escape House. It's kind of like the apartment unfaithful married men secretly own and take their mistresses to for long lunch breaks. There will be no mistresses and no infidelity in our Escape House, but there will be women. Wandering in one at a time. We will, in fact, be taking ourselves. This Escape House will be one we, and maybe three other friends, own in whatever city we all decide to live in. At the moment it is in New York City because we are in our twenties, and if you can't dream big in your twenties, when can you? It will be a secret little One Bedder Oasis with great light and a bath. It must have a bath. And we will book in our days and nights there like a timeshare, when we need space for a night, or three. When we need to take a break from the daily hum of our regular lives or space from our relationships. When we need to find time for *me* away from *us*. From whatever *us* we are in, whatever *us* looks like. It will not be because we don't love that relationship or that person. It will be because we love ourselves. And sometimes, just sometimes, you need to take space from everything else and give back to yourself. To come back to yourself. For a night, or three.

I am in Escape House 1.0 right now. This friend I told you about, I am in her apartment. This friend is away, and until we can afford a One Bedder Oasis with great light and a bath in New York City on top of our own apartments (which we still cannot afford), we must settle for each other's rented homes in Sydney. Taking space when the other takes a holiday. She is away for three days, so I am here, alone, writing, reading, and thinking about nothing else but this book and myself. Because writing, reading, and thinking is what I like to do but it is also, always, the thing that brings me back to me. And that is always the point, as Joan Didion explained.

Joan Didion and I both like to keep a notebook. Not a journal, a notebook. Didion claims to be terrible at writing down her daily or weekly account, and so do I. My journal remains shut until one spare Sunday each month when I feel compelled to mindlessly unload my feelings. But my notebook is an entirely different story. My notebook is opened daily, like I imagine Didion's is. To write down what I see, in order to work it out. In her 1968 collection of essays *Slouching Towards Bethlehem*, there is one called 'On Keeping A Notebook', in which she explains why she wrote down random accounts she witnessed or overheard. As she questioned why it was relevant to write down the accounts of strangers, she discovered she had no real interest in what one stranger said to another, but what these conversations revealed about *her*. And when I read this, I realised that the random accounts I write down are captured with exactly the same intention.

For me, The Notebook and The Escape House are similar in what they offer: a place to spend time alone in, to write in, to come back to myself. They are both destinations serving up a single solution to a desired outcome: as Didion says, to 'remember what it was to be; that is always the point'. The act of doing is always much bigger than the action itself. It is a form of self-preservation and demonstrates a willingness to grow. And that is what we are here to talk about.

You know the things you like to do, don't you? You might like to run. You might like to swim. You might like to draw. You might like to eat frozen raspberries covered in Ice Magic on the couch alone. Whatever it is, whether it is coffee with yourself once a week or finger painting on Sundays, you like to do something. Because you do it. And do you know what tends to happen when you meet a man whose company is all consuming? You stop. We have all done it. I have done it. But we must, eventually, come back to ourselves. Because you know who that man fell in love with? You. And you are a sum of the things you do.

The Doing Things Principle

There is an activewear company called Outdoor Voices whose tagline is #DoingThings. It is an excellent tagline that makes an excellent hashtag, so it appears on their hats and change-room mirrors. If I could buy you all a hat with this tagline as a daily reminder to keep doing things, I would. But I can't, so we will settle for a principle instead. This principle is the doing things principle, which is intended to keep you doing the things that make you, you.

Right now, whether you are in a relationship or you are single or it's complicated, consider the things you love doing. It may be listening to records with a glass of red wine or reading on the couch for two hours every Sunday morning or that weekly finger-painting session you don't tend to broadcast. It doesn't have to be perfect, it doesn't have to be 'right'. You just have to have an idea of the things you like to do, and figure out how you can work them into your week. It might be a matter of doing one of them four times a week, like that run. It might be a matter of doing one of them once a week, like that reading session on the couch. Schedule them in.

You also might aspire to do other, much harder, things. Maybe that is finally sitting the bar exam, or starting that novel, or creating that direct-to-consumer jewellery business that has lingered in your mind for long enough. Don't let them fade into your past. Start. Whether you finish them will be an entirely different story, but start *doing* something to move that aspiration forward and see where it leads you. It may lead you to exactly where you imagined, or take a different turn entirely. The point is to carve out some time to invest in these aspirations, because they are a part of who you are, and they will move you forward if you act on them.

And each week, regardless of whether or not you do them (though I hope you do), return to a point where you've made the space to check in with yourself. This does not have to be for long; it can be for five minutes. The point is not the amount of time. The point is you are making five minutes of your week about your relationship with yourself. Because it deserves five minutes. This small act not only gives you permission to spend five minutes with yourself. It gives you the opportunity to check in with yourself, and assess whether you are doing the small things you love to do, and the big things you aspire to do. There is a flow-on effect, of accountability and permission. It is a small act you take with you every week no matter where you are or whom you are with; no matter whether your relationship has fallen apart or whether you have just entered one. You need this small act, especially when you have just entered one. You need this reminder to remain yourself and continue taking up space in the world through the things you do, while you are falling in love with someone and they are falling in love with you. Because that is what they are falling for. Precisely you.

When You Drop What You Love, You Lose Much More

So often for women, when we enter a relationship, the excitement of the relationship causes us to want to spend every minute in it, and as a result we stop doing the things we love to do. I am not talking about our friendships here, but the things we enjoy on an intrinsic level—our interests—whether it be writing or running or reading or that aforementioned direct-to-consumer jewellery business. Our interests begin to evolve into our boyfriends' interests, and our lives begin to emulate theirs. We lose the selves that entered the relationship, and the relationship becomes an imbalanced one because of it. Their interests take priority, because we have not prioritised our own— and in doing so, we hand over our power. Sometimes this can occur with roles reversed, but for women, this is an all too familiar story. As we have seen, socialisation suggests we should take the back seat in relationships, so when we fall, hard, we sometimes do it to ourselves before the relationship has fully formed. And soon we're doing what *they* love to do, hanging out with *their* friends, moving into *their* house, and investing in our love with them while they continue to invest in themselves, and one day we wake up to realise our lives have simply been molded into the reflection of the man beside us, and our individual desires have disappeared.

So, why would we let go of what we love and what we do, now, at the start of a relationship, before there are any contesting commitments? We shouldn't and we won't. Because the foundation you form at the beginning of a relationship is exactly that—a foundation. It sets the ground rules, and the parameters, and the expectations we make of each other. And if your boyfriend expects his ambitions and interests to be more important than yours because you let yours go now, he will assume the same down the track when the housework needs to be done or a child needs to be fed. When he's busy playing the guitar or golf or finishing up something at work or going for a surf, so could you just take care of it? Don't give him the head start. Don't make things more difficult for yourself. But most importantly, don't lose yourself. Because you lose so much more. It could, in fact, be him. Remember, the man you are in a relationship with was drawn to you because of your interests, and the things you do that make you, you. Losing them can sometimes mean losing yourself, and eventually—if you lose so much of yourself he can't recognise the woman he fell in love with—you may lose him as well.

Do Teammate Love a Favour. Do You.

Teammate Love is Teammate Love because you are team-mates. It is as simple and as complicated as that. One of you may have the ball at times, and then pass it back to the other at times, but you work together the entire time. You are equal across the board. You are a team that works well together *because* you are individuals with unique strengths. So, do the team a favour and do you. It is not hurting the team, it is helping. The team wants two strong teammates, not a weak one reliant on the other. By doing you, and encouraging him to do him, you both foster the individual strengths you bring to the team to make it better. To make it work. When one of you loses these strengths, the team loses too.

On Saturdays, I write. For four hours or so. I have done this for a few years now, because that is what I like to do. That is how I like to move myself forward, and over time, writing has become what makes me feel like me. Whether it is a notebook or an article or a book, it doesn't matter. What matters is getting the words down. The man I live with knows I must write on Saturdays. Because it makes me, me, and it will continue to. It is, in part, what he loves about me even when he is frustrated that I've taken over the entire double desk and refused to join him at the beach until midday.

Four times a week, I run. Sometimes this man comes along, sometimes he doesn't, but it isn't about him. It is about me and what I need, and what I need is to run. The therapist said so and I like following the therapist's orders because she tends to be right. So, I run, for the endorphins and my general wellbeing, and I come back after this run feeling fairly upbeat. This, in turn, is good for my relationship because I feel good and am therefore good to the relationship. When I don't run four times a week, because I am human and sometimes humans avoid doing what is beneficial for themselves, I am not upbeat. I am therefore not good to the relationship, because I am grumpy. So, I am told to go for a run. And just like I have my runs, he has his surfs, which he must do at least once a week otherwise I tell him to go for a surf. That surf does not just benefit him, but me, because I cohabitate with someone in a far better mood.

Having your own shit that you keep on doing in a relationship is inextricably linked to 'Know What You Want, and Talk About It'. And the woman who told us that it is crucial to own our stories in that chapter, also learned the value of reinvesting in herself again and again within almost three decades of marriage. In her book *Becoming*, Michelle Obama wrote about going to couples' therapy with her husband, Barack. Reflecting on this later with Oprah as part of Oprah's *2020 Vision* tour,

Obama said couples' therapy taught her that she was responsible for her own happiness. 'My disappointments were about what I thought he should be doing for me, giving to me, when I hadn't really done the work to figure out what did I want?' she told the crowd. 'I had to . . . start thinking about how to carve out the life that I wanted for myself . . . And the more I did that, the more I succeeded in defining myself, for myself, the better I was in my partnership.'

We are a sum of the things we do, and so often what we do quietly states where we want to go and the life we want to lead. If we continue to take those quiet moments to ourselves, to check in with ourselves, and carve out the time to invest in what we like to do, it more often than not leads us to who we want to become. As the musician Paul Kelly taught the average Australian, *from little things, big things grow,* and if you ignore those small moments in your life when a relationship arrives, you may miss opportunities that lead you to who you want to be.

So, have your own shit, and keep doing it when you're in a relationship, and it could not only lead you to the little piece of earth you want to claim, but it will make you a happier, more fulfilled person along the way. You will be better to the partnership for it, and a better teammate for it. As Michelle Obama told Oprah and the crowd:

'If I'm going to show up equal in this partnership, I have to be able to make myself happy.'

So, remember to always come back to yourself, and remember what it is to be you. That is always the point.

Chapter 13

Diversify Your Love

If you haven't heard of Paulette Perhach, you may have heard of a Fuck Off Fund. If neither rings a bell, let me enlighten you on both. Perhach coined the term in a 2016 essay published by *The Billfold* titled 'A Story of a Fuck Off Fund', which quickly went viral. Ever since then, women, young and old, have slowly been building their own Fuck Off Funds. The idea is simple: you open a savings account and stash away enough money to keep life running relatively smoothly should you decide to depart your current situation. It could be three thousand dollars or fifteen thousand, but three to six months' pay is generally regarded as an appropriate figure. The point is exactly as the name suggests: it allows you to Fuck Off.

When Perhach penned the article, she told the story of a woman who had recently graduated university and was trying to make her way in this busy world. She had secured her first job, but student loans were holding her back and the shine of corporate life had her spending her hard-earned money like she had a corner office. But she did not. She had a slightly dodgy boss who instead made inappropriate remarks about her appearance, and a boyfriend who was showing signs of a temper but was also providing shelter. And as she worked and worked and fell further and further into debt, she could not only *not* get ahead, she could *not* leave her terrible situation, either at home or in the office, because she did not have the financial means to. She was not liberated. She was trapped.

Perhach then retold this story. It was the same story, except this woman lived within her means, copped the reality she was not—for lack of a better word—a baller, and saved. Eventually, she had the equivalent of six months' pay. So, when her boss attempted to grope her, she told him to (you guessed it) Fuck Off, and marched herself to the HR department knowing that if she wasn't supported she could support herself until she found another job. When an argument with her boyfriend grew heated, and he grabbed her wrist, she told him to (you guessed it) Fuck Off, and booked herself into a hotel. There, she searched for a new apartment, a new job, and a life upgraded on her own choices and savings account. That is a better story. That is the story women are now saving for.

The story of the Fuck Off Fund is a lesson in diversification, in power and agency, in the value of a foundation and in the importance of a safety net. Not because you will always need to use it. Because you know it is there *if* you need to use it. It gives you the ability to make greater choices. And these lessons are just as important in love as in wealth.

Your Emotional Fuck Off Fund

Friendship is a funny thing. Particularly in the age of the internet. You may have 1500 friends on Facebook (if you still have Facebook), and maybe more on Instagram. As life continues, you build collections of friends. Friends collected from high school. Friends collected from university. Friends collected in Job Number One. Job Number Two. Job Number Three. Friends collected in your early twenties, before your quarter-life crisis hit, and friends collected post quarter-life crisis, and so on. It becomes increasingly overwhelming, so I have found consolation in the science.

Oxford University evolutionary psychologist and anthropologist Robin Dunbar knows all about the psychology of friendship. Dunbar has studied it for many years, and through his time he has discovered the number of friendships the human brain can handle: 150. Our brain should be able to recognise 5000 faces (which explains our social media connections) but it can only maintain 150 friendships.

Now, this doesn't mean you can have 150 best friends. These 150 friendships are broken down into intimacy levels. The first level is your core group. Think of them as your foundation. This consists of about five close friends, which can include family. The second level is your most important social group, which consists of about fifteen people including your First Five. Beyond The First Five and The Second Fifteen, you have thirty-five friends before entering Acquaintance Territory. So, your final 100 will be acquaintances, people you run into at parties or the coffee shop, whom you say a happy hello to before a brief conversation ensues and you both move on with your days.

This is all your brain can handle. It's certainly all my brain can handle.

So, when you enter a romantic relationship it, of course, shifts the dynamic of your friendships because you are spending *a lot* of time with a new human who—depending on how your time is spent together—will soon enter your First Five. On average, Dunbar says, we lose two friendships every time we enter a new relationship. This is so common because of two reasons. We either abandon some friends because this New Person takes priority, or our values and schedules change and we subsequently lose compatibility with certain friends. We have changed, and therefore our friendships must adapt to this new version of ourselves. This is not the end of the world. This is common. It doesn't make it any easier, but the territory you should try to avoid is territory beyond the commonly experienced. Territory where you lose your entire First Five due to a new relationship.

So, how do we avoid this?

We build our Emotional Fuck Off Fund, and we invest in it. Then reinvest in it. Consistently. So, consider your First Five. Who are the five most important people in your life? Then consider your Second Fifteen. Who are the fifteen people who make the cut? Invest in all of these people where you can, but we are here to talk mainly about your First Five.

Those five names who currently take priority in your life are those you need to keep reinvesting in whenever a man enters your life. Because this is the time you will need your First Five more than ever. Even if it doesn't feel like it's the case in the early stages of your New! Enthralling! Glossy! Love! Story! Because this story will go one of two ways. It will end in A Glorious Mess at some point. Or it will go another way, which I will discuss on later pages. If your love story ends in A Glorious Mess, as many relationships in your life will, you will need your First Five to help support you through the grief. They are your foundation of human connection that will carry you through the moments you cannot walk through alone. They are the five people you will be able to lean on, confide in, laugh with, when you need someone to lean on or confide in or laugh with. So, invest in your First Five, spend quality time with them, check in with them, and be there for them when they need you. Of course, your First Five will change, and this will likely happen when you enter a relationship. Sometimes you will need to amend or update the list. But you will always have and will always need to invest in your First Five. They are your Emotional Fuck Off Fund, as Lauren will now portray in a fake but believable story.

Lauren is a lawyer who has lived in New York City for seven years. She has her First Five, which has of course changed during her time in New York City because it is life, and friendships evolve with it. In March, she meets a man on Hinge and they go on a date. It's a case of instant attraction. Their interests are aligned. They both love badminton and Scrabble and weekends out of the city, because this is a fake story, so why not have fun with it? They spend every weekend out of the city playing badminton and Scrabble, and Lauren doesn't see her First Five on weekends anymore. That is fine because she can see them during the week, but she doesn't do that either. She spends every night at her Badminton Lover's apartment and by September, her First Five are gone. She hasn't reinvested her time in any new friendships either, so it's not a case of her First Five evolving. The list is wide open. And then she finds a text. Badminton Lover left his phone open and a text popped up from Sandra, his colleague. Lauren opens it, and then another, and then many, many more. Badminton Lover has been having an affair.

Lauren can't confide in anyone about it, so when she confronts Badminton Lover he talks her off the ledge. He convinces her she has it all wrong. She misinterpreted it. And because Lauren has not confided in anyone else, she believes him. She has nowhere to go anyway. No one knows about it but her. Maybe she can get past it? So, she spends the night, and a week passes. She moves past it, enough to stay in the relationship, but she hasn't processed it properly because no reliable friend has forced her to confront it. Trust is gone, respect has dissipated. Yet the relationship continues, and Badminton Lover keeps taking advantage of what appears to be a very forgiving girlfriend. He continues his bad behaviour while Lauren's self-esteem is broken down to a point where she is so weak, she doesn't know herself anymore. So, she stays. She has nowhere to go and no one to talk any sense into her.

And that is enough of that depressing story. Let's rewind and insert the Emotional Fuck Off Fund.

Lauren is a lawyer who has lived in New York City for seven years. She has her First Five, which has of course changed during her time in New York City because it is life, and friendships evolve with it. In March, she meets a man on Hinge and they go on a date. It's a case of instant attraction. Their interests are aligned. They both love badminton and Scrabble and weekends out of the city, because this is still a fake story, so why not have fun with it? They spend every weekend out of the city playing badminton and Scrabble, and Lauren doesn't see her First Five on weekends. That is fine because she can see them during the week, and she does. She spends a couple of nights a week at dinner with her First Five. Not together. Separately most of the time, but sometimes they all meet. She loses one friend on her list because her values have changed and they don't click in the same way they once did. This friend slides down the list, into her Second Fifteen. This is fine, though, because she has grown close to a new colleague at work, who soon makes it into her First Five. And then she finds a text. Badminton Lover left his phone open and a text popped up from Sandra, his colleague. Lauren opens it, and then another, and then many, many more. Badminton Lover has been having an affair.

Lauren calls Number Two in her First Five. They meet at a bar, talk it through, and make a plan. Lauren meets Badminton Lover at his house and he tries to talk her off the ledge. She tells him to Fuck Off, packs up her stuff and catches a cab home to her apartment. Where Number Two is waiting with a tub of ice-cream, and Lauren cries in her arms all night. The next morning is hard, and so are the next few weeks. But Lauren spends her weekends with her First Five, in the city for some and on weekenders for others. After a few months, she moves on.

That is a better story, and a lesson in diversifying your love. As with all diversification, it diversifies your risk. You don't want to invest all of your earnings (love) into one asset (Badminton Lover). You want to spread out the risk and leave yourself with an emotional safety net. You want an Emotional Fuck Off Fund, a diversified account with a certain amount of love stashed there to keep your life running relatively smoothly should you decide to depart your current romantic situation. The point is exactly as the name suggests: it allows you to Fuck Off if your romantic relationship ends, and it liberates you when you do. But it is also there, in case your relationship survives.

If your romantic relationship does not end in A Glorious Mess at some point, it will end in Happily Ever After, In A Happy But Sometimes Tricky Ever After Kind Of Way. Because relationships, like life, are not always happy, no matter how good they are. There are the good chapters and the bad. Sometimes the chapter is a fulfilling one. Sometimes it is hard and you cannot see the light, but you get through it because you love the other person. And then you look back, with them, and you can see where one chapter ended and the other started. But one person— one relationship—is not the answer to emotional support in all the different chapters of your life. No one person in your First Five has the answer to everything. Even your girlfriend with the ice-cream stash. And when you place the weight of that expectation on a romantic partner, your relationship is not as fulfilling as it could be. Because you are coming from a place of need rather than a place of want. You *need* them to have the answer. You *need* them to support you in everything. And they cannot possibly do this, because they are a human. Not a village.

Your Emotional FOF Is Your Village

You know the saying: It takes a village to raise a child. I don't think this changes as we age. We still need our village. Belgian psychotherapist Esther Perel knows this, and believes we cannot look to our romantic partner to fulfil the support a village once provided. In her TED Talk on 'The secret to desire in a long-term relationship', she claimed that in modern relationships and marriage, we have never expected more from our partners than we do now, and we also live longer. We expect this one other person to be everything for us, all at once: 'Give me belonging, give me identity, give me continuity, but give me transcendence and mystery and awe all in one,' she said. 'Give me comfort, give me edge. Give me novelty, give me familiarity. Give me predictability, give me surprise. And we think it's a given.'

We now ask something of our romantic relationships that we never have before. We ask (and expect) all of the above emotional support. The reality is, one person cannot give us that. But our First Five can. Not so much romantic desire, but the emotional foundation to feel a sense of belonging and awe, and comfort and edge, and novelty and familiarity, and predictability and surprise.

The man we stumble upon who can give us Teammate Love probably cannot give us all of those things. So, we accept the emotional support he can give us and find the other emotional support we desire (and maybe even need) elsewhere—in our friendships. Your First Five should be able to fulfil this. And if not, look beyond your First Five into your Second Fifteen. Invest away.

Research from Northwestern University titled 'Emotionships: Examining People's Emotion-Regulation Relationships and Their Consequences for Well-Being' showed that people who diversified their emotional needs across multiple people instead of depending on one person—or 'the one'—had greater overall life satisfaction. The study's authors encouraged people to develop multiple 'emotionships', claiming that those who diversified their emotions between a range of people presented higher wellbeing than counterparts who may have had the same number of close relationships, but didn't diversify their emotions between them.

I have a friend I go to for creative inspiration, and I always walk away from our chats fulfilled. I have a friend I can go to when I need to divulge my darkest feelings, and she understands, because she feels them too. I have a friend I go to who is the most caring force I have ever seen, and I need her superpower sometimes. I have friends I go to for a good laugh. I have friends I go to for brutal honesty when I need to hear it but don't necessarily want to. My teammate cannot give me all of that, nor would I want him to. I cannot give all of that to him either, so he invests away in his Emotional Fuck Off Fund, as he should. It's good for the both of us.

Your Village Enables You to Come From a Place of Want, Not a Place of Need

When your love is diversified across your village and your Emotional Fuck Off Fund is intact, you not only enter, but stay, in relationships with a different intention. You come from a place of want, not a place of need, which allows you to behave differently. You are kinder to the relationship, because you want to be there. You are disappointed less often, because the weight of unrealistic expectations has not been put solely onto one other human. You argue better, because you pick your fights and take the ones you don't pick to your girlfriends and you vent. You stay in the relationship, because you want to be there, not because you need to. You are a better teammate for this, and your relationship is better for it. Maybe most importantly, your friendships are too.

Over the course of a lifetime you will make 396 friends, but only thirty-three will last. So, don't beat yourself up when you lose some along the way. This will most often occur when you enter a relationship. You will lose those two friendships, and maybe more. I certainly did. And I beat myself up about it. Diversifying my love has been a lesson I've learned along the way and I have not always got it right. In fact, I've learned this lesson because I got it wrong.

I entered a relationship and within six months our brief overseas holiday had turned into a temporary twelve-month move. All of a sudden, I was living in another country with my teammate but without my First Five or Second Fifteen. I had also neglected them before I left. I had been working night shifts in a news room as well as being distracted by the shine of a new love. So, I walked through a year of self-actualisation with mainly this new love by my side. And as enriching as it was, it was also a deadweight on the relationship, because there were too many expectations. Too much dependency. Too much need. And I returned home to rebuild my

First Five and Second Fifteen. And the relationship I am in—which is the same relationship—feels like it is now in a completely different chapter. We survived the last, but lessons were learned and new and old friendships have been built and rebuilt since then.

So, if you slip in the shine of a new love, don't beat yourself up. When you wake up on a cold, lonely day to realise you've let some loves go, don't dwell. Reconnect. And build your First Five back up again. My love has been diversified again, and I am not only a better friend for it but a better teammate. I am also a better, stronger person, because I am walking through each day from a place of want. Not a place of need. And I hold all my loves to a higher standard for it.

Chapter 14

New Game, New Wins

The thing that makes love such a fascinating subject is that it is inextricably linked to power. One person will always love the other person more, and while that power imbalance may change between parties each day or month or year, the imbalance always exists. For so long, women have focused on wielding that power in a relationship because we had no power outside of it. The social and economic constructs of society always favoured man, so we used love to wield power in whatever way we could. We searched for men who loved us more than we loved them, and did whatever we needed to ensure they continued loving us more. This was a necessity for our survival, but as social and economic constructs are changing to move closer toward equality, our focus has remained on wielding that power in love, and it has had a destructive side effect.

Where we have channelled our focus has indirectly reinforced the message that we must find and wield the love of a man to have any success in this world, and all it has given us is anxiety. So much so, by the time we find a man, we are just so excited that someone loves us we often compromise our lives to keep it. Romantic and dating literature of our time has maintained women's focus on securing a man, and as a result we forgot that we might actually want more from men. Our lives are very different to those of our unliberated grandmothers, so we do not have to channel our focus where they did. In fact, it should be channelled in the opposite direction. Instead of finding success through a relationship, we now require the right relationship to back our success. We don't require love, we require the *right* love. That is what we must remember and demand.

I have written this book with the assumption that the person you choose—who will, I hope, give you Teammate Love—will be one of the biggest influences in your success. They will influence it for better, or for worse. When you jump on Bumble and swipe right, when you connect with some handsome stranger in the coffee shop, you don't know what the future holds with this person. You may go on one date and it is a flop; you may end up together for two years and part ways; you may end up together for the rest of your lives and one day walk down the aisle toward this handsome man who will become your handsome husband. You don't know where each romance that enters your life will go, but it is likely one of them will result in a future. It is therefore important you greet each one with an understanding of what this future holds and what you need to do to protect yourself along the way. What follows is an overview of where Teammate Love will lead you in this future, and an examination of the gendered pressures that still exist at every point.

A Relationship of Real Negotiation (and Equal Love)

'I think we're really engaged in a seachange,' Stephanie Coontz told me when we discussed the evolution of romantic partnerships. 'Toward one in which we're beginning to learn how to make equality—and I don't mean sameness, but real equality and real negotiation—exciting and erotic and a basis of love. And by negotiation I don't mean the sort of compromises women make internally to avoid arguments or hurt feelings, but the real give and take that gets both people's needs met.'

The relationship a teammate will give you is one where real negotiation will occur. With this comes equal compromise and, as a result, the chance for equal success. It is not, as it has been throughout history, a relationship where the man can continue to take and the woman continually compromises her career, or the success she hoped for. It is a relationship where professional success and love can coexist for women, as it currently does for men. This environment of real negotiation, built on equality, allows you to continue being yourself and avoid compromising who you are. It also creates a more satisfied, happier relationship for you and the man you choose as your teammate.

Equal relationships have not always been the most satisfying, and now we're not only seeing more men and women wanting them, but that the men and women who have them are actually happier. 'Equal partnerships,' Michael Flood said, 'have more trusting, intimate and more connected relationships, so with genuine gender equality comes greater communication, greater connection and so on.' Traditional gender roles limit intimacy and connection in relationships. 'If you've got two highly traditional people . . . you can have very low levels of communication and very low levels of disclosure. He's not communicating because he's a very traditional man and "that's not what real men do", and she's not communicating because "she should put her needs second" and make sure her husband comes first, and so on. So, traditional gender roles are bad on both sides.'

Since marriage equality has been established across the majority of the western world, we are also now learning from same-sex couples who do not face the same gendered challenges in marriage. They have fought harder to have the legal right to marry, but within modern marriage they are now showing us the way.

Heterosexual marriages have traditionally been based on the man having greater authority than the woman, and a division of tasks based upon gender. This makes it more difficult for heterosexual couples to evolve beyond this view, and into a marriage that better suits our modern lives. Recent research from the Population Research Center at The University of Texas at Austin led by Michael Garcia shows that same-sex couples experience lower marital stress than heterosexual couples. Most interestingly, it's not *all women* who report the highest marital distress, but *only women married to men*.

As we recast love to be based less on gendered assumption within our relationships, we are now hoping to follow in the footsteps of same-sex couples. Researchers John Gottman and Robert Levenson found that same-sex couples engage in real negotiation and handle disagreements better than heterosexual couples; over a twelve-year timeline, same-sex couples used humour and affection more often and were less hostile than heterosexual couples. They also calmed down more quickly once an argument was resolved.

If you are in an equal partnership, which cannot exist within the constraints of traditional gender roles, then your teammate will not only communicate better because the very nature of your relationship forces him to, but you will also communicate better because you treat your voice as equal and real negotiation occurs. This extends beyond general conversation, and makes its way into the bedroom also.

More Sexual Agency, and Better Sex

Research from Rutgers University in the United States showed that women who upheld feminist beliefs within their relationships had more satisfying sex lives. In the study, researchers Laurie Rudman and Julie Phelan surveyed more than 500 people, both young and old, around the general satisfaction and health of their relationships; the couples with feminist partners had 'greater sexual satisfaction'.

Flood claims women who believe they shouldn't initiate relationships do indeed have less sexual agency and often this impacts their sexual lives. 'In relationships, they are less likely to ask for what they want. They're more likely to feel like they need to focus on their partner's sexual pleasure. His sexual needs, preferences, and so on. So, they end up having shittier sex lives,' he said. 'And so, in some ways do their male partners because that kind of sexual dissatisfaction those women feel also can then flow on to the quality of the relationship.' With greater intimacy, communication and consequently connection, a more satisfying relationship exists.

Then you add the normality of real negotiation, which is essential to maintaining a more satisfying relationship, and it makes life a whole lot easier when you decide to move in together. Because the joy of moving in together brings with it all the joy of doing the dishes and the laundry and replacing the toilet-paper roll and arguing about who is the backbone of the household, which will likely still be you, but we'll do our best to avoid that.

Equal Housework, and a More Satisfied Relationship

In recent decades, doing an equal share of housework has become increasingly vital to the stability and satisfaction of a partnership. A study conducted by researchers Dan Carlson, Amanda Miller and Sharon Sassler for the Council on Contemporary Families in the United States analysed marriages from 1992 to 2006. What it revealed was that in marriages formed before 1992, couples were fairly happy with the woman bearing the brunt of housework but by 2006, everything had changed. The couples who shared the housework most equally had happier, more satisfied relationships than those in traditional partnerships. So, while your mother may have shouldered the burden of housework, and had a better relationship for it, you will not.

Today, women who do the predominant share of housework report higher levels of discord—which is, unfortunately, a lot of women. In the aforementioned study, only one-third of couples were sharing an equal amount of housework by 2006.

This only becomes more difficult to balance once children come along (which we will explore in later pages).

With Teammate Love by your side, you have the greatest chance to join the one-third of couples who were sharing the housework equally in 2006. And if you suddenly feel yourself bearing the brunt of it when you move in, negotiate your way into a fairer share. And if all that fails, there is a final route you can take, and it involves being unexceptional.

Tip! An Unexceptional Theory

I have a general theory on the keeping of a house, and that is to maintain being fairly unexceptional at it. I am not bad at it but I am also not very good at it either, and there is some logic for this. As Nora Ephron wrote in *Heartburn*, 'My mother was a good recreational cook, but what she basically believed about cooking was that if you worked hard and prospered, someone else would do it for you.'

Until I can afford this, which I likely won't, I have to maintain my baseline level of not very good. And I have a good reason for this, which I consolidated in a taxi trip a few years ago. I found myself in the standard place I find myself—arguing for women's basic human rights—with my driver, and when I made my final point he countered it with, 'But women are just better at cleaning and raising kids.' I argued women are better at it because we, as an entire gender, have spent more time doing it and as the old adage goes, *practice makes perfect*. Then a revelation arrived: what if we stopped being better?

As you know, I do not have kids, but I do have a small apartment I share with a fairly tall man who is better at cooking, better at cleaning, and better at 'styling a home' (his words, not mine)—and I like to keep it this way. I am fortunate to have inherited his baseline level of good, but that is not the point. The point is I have actively chosen to maintain my baseline level of not very good. That way he can never throw the taxi driver's argument in my face because my counter will be, 'Well, *I'm not.*'

But the caveat here is the role that assumption, and therefore expectation, play in this game. He does not expect or assume I will clean and cook more than he does, because I am not better at it than him, nor do I enjoy it any more than he does. So, we divide it up and cook on alternate nights and do the shopping together, and it has never really slipped, until it did.

I was at home on Fridays writing this book, so in breaks or moments of procrastination, I would clean the apartment. Soon, four weeks had passed and I had cleaned the apartment every Friday. As a result, I became grumpy. So, we sat down and had a conversation about it and he said he was becoming conscious of it too and then we both made an effort, and then it slipped again. I had started to nag, which never works, and then I remembered my theory. And I stopped cleaning. The mess built up and then on one fine day, the sun beamed in and he started cleaning the apartment because it was unlivable. So, I started cleaning as well, and—because we did it together—soon enough the apartment was clean.

This outcome teaches us this: people take shortcuts. My boyfriend knew the apartment was being cleaned, so he didn't bother trying. If I were in his shoes, I probably would have had a crack at it too because people are inherently lazy. We're also busy and most of us don't like doing unpaid work because it is, well, unpaid. Hence, we do what we can to avoid it.

So, if you move in with a man, have the conversation, establish the ground rules, divide up the work and, if you can, do it together. And if he starts to slip, have the conversation again. If you start to slip, expect him to have the same conversation with you. Because you are team-mates. If that doesn't work, start being unexceptional at it and eventually, someone will have to cave—try not to let it be you.

If your relationship is based on a foundation of real negotiation, it will be normal to have the conversation, and it will be assumed more conversations will ensue when someone slips. Of course it will ebb and flow, because lives are not straight lines, but the point is you can have the conversation. And when the conversation fails, resort to not being very good.

Farewelling Resentment and the Old 'Ball and Chain'

As shared housework has risen to improve relationship satisfaction for couples, and we are working toward women's professional fulfillment being seen as equally valuable as men's, we are slowly, I hope, seeing a change in the stereotype of what it means to be a 'wife'. I am not talking here just about the role she will play as she works and raises children on a more even keel with her husband, but the changing stereotype of her general satisfaction with the whole 'wife' thing. 'Historically, women have been less than happy with the inequality in marriages,' Coontz told me, quoting studies that show that when men are more engaged fathers, they're actually happier than when their wife does the majority of parenting. When men take an active role in raising their children, they 'feel the same kind of rewards with fathering that women get with mothering', but there is also the simple fact that men who share the load feel happier because 'it makes their wives happier'.

I sometimes struggle with the word 'wife', and the reason doesn't lie in the word 'wife' at all, but with the terms some husbands use to describe their wives. As Jia Tolentino wrote in *The New Yorker* about the history of the wife, 'Structurally speaking, the wife was controlled by her husband, but, culturally, the joke was that she controlled him.' A 1960s survey conducted by the Dictionary of American Regional English found that the most common joking terms used by American men to describe their wives included 'battle-axe', 'ball and chain', 'old lady' and 'boss'. Now, when men refer to their wives as their 'ball and chain' I ask them why they married them, because it bothers me more than people who think Smartwater makes you smart. *Dude, you literally saved up three months' pay, bought a ring, got down on one knee and asked her to be your wife. It was, at its most basic level, your call. Why are you now implying she held you hostage at the end of the aisle in a tux in front of 150 of your closest friends to say, I do?*

I say this, but I know why they do it, and so do they. They want to uphold the cultural joke that they, as men, are controlled by their wives so that when they have to leave their mates at the pub after seven beers it's not *their* fault they're leaving, it's their *wife's*.

But with the rise of Teammate Love comes the departure of an era of love based on what Coontz called 'an exchange of specialised services and behaviours' that has left the wife not particularly happy with her dealt hand. Where she nags him about the dishes, or she asks him to come home after said seven beers on a Friday because she hasn't seen him all week and her capacity for childrearing as a solo pursuit has reached its peak. Or she wakes him up early on Saturday morning, when he is hungover from those seven beers, to 'help' look after child number two while she feeds child number one because one child might be easy but two children is, well, an entirely less straightforward story. She becomes the demanding wife, the nagging wife, the ball and chain, the battle-axe, the boss, because she is asking him to do something that doesn't involve taking a Nurofen and sleeping for another three hours.

When you share similar experiences and shoulder the same burdens at a similar rate, there is less room for resentment to take hold. And also less room to diss each other. If the new-age, teammate 'wife' is a ball and chain, so is her husband. And we know men would never call themselves that, so the only route for it to take is one that disappears.

Role Modelling for Your Generation, and Then Some

Research now shows that couples with equality at the core of their relationships do, in fact, influence the couples around them. The more common it is for a couple to show equality in one area—such as a housework chore like doing the grocery shopping together—the more common it is for other couples to feel pressured to do so. So, if you exhibit Teammate Love, it is likely your friends and their boyfriends will follow suit.

As I said at the beginning, this book is *a reimagining of progress*, because each relationship built on Teammate Love will influence a large sum of people in its orbit. A few of those people may then opt for Teammate Love and influence a large sum of the people in their orbit, and so on. Teammate Love creates influence because it is a superior, more satisfied relationship than others. It is the Meghan Markle and Prince Harry kind of love. It is the Michelle and Barack Obama kind of love. It is the Marty and Ruth Bader Ginsburg kind of love. People notice that love, and then they want it for themselves.

So, they do what they can to seek it out. And slowly, over time, an entire generation might embrace this kind of love that shifts Teammate Love into the default love of our lives.

This, alone, will not create equality. It will not fix everything. But it will move some things forward. 'You're not going to create utopia in your own home, but you can create the modelling of how this works, you can use your relationship as a beacon for other people and your own kids, you can affect other people's understanding and appreciation of it,' Coontz said.

In studies of more than 100,000 men and women from twenty-nine countries, Harvard Business School's Kathleen McGinn found that girls who grew up with working mothers were more likely to be employed, hold supervisory roles, and earn higher incomes than daughters of stay-at-home mothers. They also were just as happy. The sons of working mothers contributed more to housework and childcare when they grew up. Meanwhile, researchers at the University of British Columbia found in 2014 that girls who grew up in households where their father contributed a higher share of parenting and unpaid work had higher aspirations academically and professionally, and were more likely to take on careers in traditionally male fields, such as science and tech. And we know it doesn't just benefit daughters; it also benefits sons.

Michael Flood agrees that the role modelling of parents has an immense impact on their children. 'We know from research among boys that what boys see their dads do also shapes their own identities and their own pathways and trajectories into adulthood and the kind of men they become,' Flood told me. 'When boys have seen their dads behaving non-violently and respectfully, then they are more likely to live in those same ways themselves.'

Flood pointed to research showing that when men have daughters, their support for gender equality in the workplace increases. He used this as an example of the 'two-way street' between work and home. 'It may be that the experience of having daughters makes them more aware of the constraints and challenges and every-day sexism that girls and women face. It may be that it increases their aspirations, not only for their daughters, but for girls and women in general,' Flood said. 'Given that evidence, I think it's likely that you would see flow-on effects [in the workplace].'

With each formation of Teammate Love, we can inch the world a little closer to equality. Through each rela-tionship, there are positive flow-on effects: whether that is friends witnessing Teammate Love and then desiring it for themselves; or men supporting gender equality at work more stoically because they have a love based on equality with the most important woman in their life; or through positive role modelling for our future daughters and sons, who will grow up to become women with higher aspiration and men with greater empathy.

The historically gendered expectations existing from the Marriage Bar, despite its removal, and the current research showing us that men's lives generally improve when they marry while women's lives generally do not, show us the pressures that still exist. We can move the global dial collectively with our individual relationships, but just as we can influence the world, the pressures of the world will always push back. Once you find Teammate Love, you will have a basis of love from which having difficult conversations is a normal, important thing; where real negotiation is embraced; where the give and take isn't gendered, but fair. It will always ebb and flow, and it is crucial to understand the pressures at force against you both. 'I think you can have an equal relationship but one of the ways you can most closely approach it is to understand the pressures that are there to re-create inequality at every bend,' Coontz told me. 'I don't mean that you have to be all the time examining yourself, but you have to be aware that just wanting equality or behaving that way in one area doesn't always turn over.'

Starting a family will, of course, be the biggest pressure pushing against the Teammate Love you have with your partner. The research, the statistics, the stories from every mother I have spoken to, lay this narrative down time and time again. *It's all fine, until you have kids.* In a 2015 study from the Council on Contemporary Families, researchers examined couples who both said they were egalitarian. The time studies of these couples supported their beliefs before they had a baby. A year after the birth of their first child, both the man and woman still reported completely egalitarian ways, but they were wrong. These women had not cut back at work but had increased their unpaid work and childcare while the men had not done so in the same way. They both thought their relationship was equal because they were both still working, but the mother now had two jobs. As Coontz explained to me, 'They were kidding each other that they were still egalitarian. At some point, that will probably hurt their relationship.'

In her *Quarterly Essay*, 'Men at Work', Annabel Crabb highlighted a graph composed by researcher Jennifer Baxter, from the Australian Institute of Family Studies which—again—supports this narrative. The graph demonstrates what happens to women's and men's lives when they have their first child, and shows what the following twelve years looked like. Before the arrival of their child, the average man and woman are both doing around fifteen hours of housework a week. After the birth of their first child, the father's housework remains the same while the mother's doubles. If you think it might just be for the first year, know that it is not. This arrangement remains fairly unchanged for the following twelve years. The mother's parenting hours also rise drastically from zero to forty-five hours a week in that first year—slowly tapering over the following twelve—while the father's rise to less than half of that. Meanwhile, his employment remains unchanged, kicking along steadily at around forty-five hours a week, while the mother's drops drastically in the first year, to fewer than ten. Her employment slowly rises over the following twelve years, but never returns to where it was before she had a baby. This is not an old graph. This graph was produced in 2019.

'For women, it will make a vital, long-term difference to their levels of relationship satisfaction—their levels of happiness in a long-term partnership if they can find a male partner who will pull his weight around the house, in parenting, and also in terms of those more subtle forms of emotional labour,' Michael Flood told me. 'You know, who will organise the birthday present for his daughter's friend's birthday, or who will look out for ageing parents, or who will think ahead to whether a new set of school uniforms have to be bought because that's often where inequalities are most obvious . . . So, men who can pull their weight in those ways, that makes a profound difference to women's levels of satisfaction in relationships.'

I have not given birth. I do not raise children. I do not have what society would call a conventional 'family'. So, I am not going to pretend I have any idea how to 'fix' this issue. I don't believe it is my place, and even if I did, I don't believe anyone would listen to me. All I know is this: If I have to exist in a world where I'll likely retire with half the amount of superannuation my partner retires on; and if we have children, his career will kick along fine while mine suffers as I receive the joys of shouldering the majority of unpaid work and child raising while he does a sweet fifteen hours each week; if it is more likely I will not beat these odds than beat them, I want a damn good hand to try. Because I will, hell or high water, beat them. I will not do it. I will not have it. As Kathleen Gerson's research from *Removing the Roadblocks* showed us, a lot of young women won't have it either. The study showed we would rather go it alone than have anything less than equality, anything less than Teammate Love. We don't want to be punished by marriage and child-rearing, like we have been throughout history. We don't want to be called a battle-axe or a ball and chain anymore. We're done. We want a love to back us, not hold us back, and now we know the benefits this love offers. It offers a platform of real negotiation, of a more equal and less gendered give and take throughout our lives, it offers up the opportunity to have difficult conversations when they're required.

And with this, we find ourselves in a relationship that is statistically more likely to have better communication, greater connection, better sex on offer more nights of the week. And consequently, we have a healthier, more satisfied relationship that gives us the one hope we have grasped ever so tightly in our hands for decades.

It is the hope to be limited only by ourselves. To have, above all else, a choice. To choose the course of our lives, and the pace, and everything else that comes with it. And now we will choose Teammate Love to give us that choice.

In an episode of *Oprah's Master Class*, Maya Angelou said that true love liberates, and over the course of writing this book I have grown to believe her definition of love is the definition of Teammate Love. 'Love liberates,' Angelou wisely said. 'It doesn't just hold—that's ego. Love liberates. It doesn't bind. Love says, "I love you. I love you if you're in China. I love you if you're across town. I love you if you're in Harlem. I love you. I would like to be near you. I'd like to have your arms around me. I'd like to hear your voice in my ear. But that's not possible now, so I love you. Go."'

You want that liberated love, and you now know what to do.

Go.

Chapter 15

Plan S(ingle)

About once every six weeks, I fall in love. It usually comes at a time where I am ready to fall again; after the emotional rollercoaster of the last slows to pull up, the end of the ride impending. They are all very different, I should add, but I certainly have a type. It involves a certain level of arrogance—enough to be amusing, not enough to be abrasive—dished out with a good sense of humour. They are rappers* and I often fall in love with them more than once. I get over them, of course, but within a few months I am back. Desperately knocking on the doors of their Spotify accounts.

Over the course of 2019, I fell in love—at least twice—with Childish Gambino, Chance The Rapper, Kanye West, and Jay Z (I had to rejoin Apple Music for him). The new Lion King album also resulted in a brief affair. Each great love is always intense. I don't just consume each album, each song; I watch every interview I can locate on

* I have written 'rappers' for ease, but they are, of course, much more. They are rappers, songwriters, singers, producers, record executives, entrepreneurs, actors and I could go on but I won't.

YouTube, I read every *New Yorker* and *New York Times* profile I can dig up, but maybe most importantly, I enter something far more acute. I enter their world. I start to see each encounter through their eyes, their lyrics, their stories, their songs. Their world becomes mine as I sit on my mundane commute, write at my desk, clear my inbox, and run my regular route. I listen to them like I *am* them. They are me. A small white woman, wandering through her relatively privileged life to the soundtrack of rap. I am a walking contradiction, but they can handle me. As Jay Z wrote in his autobiography, *Decoded*, 'rap is built to handle contradictions'.

These great loves orbit my world for around six weeks, maybe to return again a few months later. And for good measure, we usually do it all over again. But the greatest of all my great loves last year, the woman I have returned to time and time again, is Lizzo. I was introduced to her through a friend, who sent me the link to Lizzo's first major-label release, *Cuz I Love You*, and I paid attention. I was instructed to listen to 'Tempo' featuring Missy Elliott first. It was love at first listen. I was hooked. I consumed the entire album from start to finish three times that day. I shared her with friends. I always do.

And then the research began. The fourteen-track album, which was not her first, debuted at number six on the Billboard 200 chart. It went to number one on iTunes, and the critics adored it. A Detroit-born singer was having her breakthrough moment at age thirty. I was cheering her on from the sidelines. Three months before I found her, in February, Allison P. Davis had beaten me to it in her profile of Lizzo for *The Cut*. I will never forget the headline. 'It's Just a Matter of Time Till Everybody Loves Lizzo,' she wrote, and she was right.

Now everybody does love Lizzo. I have had to share my greatest love with the entire world, and it is an honour. She has performed on every possible talk show. She graces ads, and stars in memes. She has become culture. She came out of a giant wedding cake at the BET awards, she performed in front of a huge inflatable arse at the VMAs, and her consistent message of self-love has reverberated around the world. See, the subtitle that followed *The Cut*'s headline is the most important part of Lizzo's story. What followed 'It's Just a Matter of Time Till Everybody Loves Lizzo,' was the subtitle, 'as much as she loves herself'.

The message Lizzo sends is her superpower. It is more than a mission statement. It is a consistent affirmation told and retold through each note, each word, each song, each flute solo, each '*Bitch!*', each performance. It isn't one album. It isn't one genre. It is a way of life, and Lizzo is living it. We are familiar with this way of life but it is not one we are used to seeing women live. The men we see living it are usually rappers, and it is part of the reason I fall for them. The narrative of their music sewn together with an arrogance that persuades you into believing they can do anything, while they rap about their pitfalls. You trust them. They have an ease in themselves despite their flaws. Confidence of the casual sort. And through their music, you slowly start to believe you have this ease, this arrogance, this confidence too. Some would argue Beyoncé has this. But Beyoncé does something different. She will tell us we run the world, but she exhibits this with a sense of control. A public display of perfection, even when she is mad and destroying a car with a baseball bat.

Lizzo does not exhibit a sense of control or a sense of perfection. She exhibits an entirely different force. She is free. She vows to love herself in every instance of her life, even the messy ones. In fact, she seems to love herself more in these moments. There is no filter to her music. She makes it okay to feel shit about yourself, and love yourself anyway. There is no 'I will be happy once I have achieved *this*'; 'I will be beautiful once I have lost *this*'; 'I will be whole once I have found *this*'. Rather, it is: 'I am *here*, bitch.'

'I am a pioneer in creating modern self-love, body-positive music,' she said in *The Cut* profile. Her lyrical takes on modern self-help have caused every third woman in the summer of 2019 to publicly declare that they too were *100 per cent that bitch*. But her words have had an impact far greater and wider than the average woman's Instagram caption, and the impact lies in a crucial nuance. The single factor that makes Lizzo such a pioneer, as Allison P. Davis wrote, is that, 'Lizzo has been teaching herself to be 100 per cent that bitch since she was Melissa Jefferson, a self-described dorky, overweight preteen'. She's not a Victoria's Secret model preaching self-care or an Instagram influencer explaining her ten-step skin-care routine. She hasn't had an easy life or journey to this moment, where the entire world is now paying attention to Lizzo.

She continues to work on her relationship with herself. She goes to therapy. She quotes her own lyrics back to herself in times of need. She has cancelled shows when she's reached a point where she isn't taking care of herself. In her profile with *The Cut*, Lizzo said she's embracing the 'body-positive' title but does not want to label herself this way. It is simply her existence, not a hashtag or an act. 'I say I love myself, and they're like, "Oh my gosh, she's so brave. She's so political,"' she said. 'Even when body positivity is over, it's not like I'm going to be a thin white woman. I'm going to be black and fat. That's just hopping on a trend and expecting people to blindly love themselves. That's fake love. I'm trying to figure out how to actually live it.'

Her music is a celebration of the lifestyle of loving yourself, and now the entire world wants to join the party. And it's had me thinking about why we're all so hooked, about what we've been missing out on.

A Love Worthy of Dom Pérignon

For women, the moments worthy of celebration in our lives do not by and large involve purely—and only—ourselves. When you think about the milestones prompting public recognition and registries and invites we stick to our fridges for too many months, they recognise, mainly, marriage. Perhaps the engagement beforehand, and then, possibly, the baby showers that follow. But predominantly marriage. Our greatest celebration in life is still, really, the wedding. And when this celebration occurs, when your friends and family unite to toast to a love that has formed and the promises that have been made, something else happens. A new chapter is recognised, and as a result, begins. Your emergence into adulthood occurs. Your adult life starts. It is acknowledged by your people, and you merrily step into your future with your husband by your side. But if your celebration has not yet taken place, if your emergence into adulthood has not yet arrived, these celebrations exist as constant reminders that you are not there yet. The message is reinforced again and again.

You are, still, a work in progress.

This assumption is reinforced throughout teenagehood with the mothers who see their daughters as successful when they find a 'nice boyfriend'. And then later in our twenties, when brunch with friends is served with conversation revolving around the men we are speaking to. And in our thirties and basically every decade following, when single women are asked whether they have had any 'joy' on the dating front. Men are asked who they are banging; women are asked if they have found someone yet, as if their lives depend on it. These questions are littered with the patriarchal socialisation and assumption that a woman is only successful, is only whole, is only adult, once she has found a man to spend the rest of her life with. A man who will open the doors to this new chapter, allowing his loved one to emerge into adulthood as she twirls into her new house, which is finally a home, and the prospects of a puppy, dinner parties and 2.5 children. She has finally arrived at her destination. She is whole. She is free.

When in actual truth, women freed themselves from this storyline a long time ago. The only problem is the constraints of longstanding cultural norms—of what is considered right and wrong, good and bad, adult and not adult—still try to lure us back into traditional trajectories through questions, assumptions and celebrations of a love deemed worthy of a glass of Dom Pérignon.

The love we share with someone else. It makes women feel like they haven't emerged into adulthood until they arrive at this celebration, even when this story—that forces so many women to settle—is an outdated one.

The 'Single Positive' Revolution and Rise in Self-Partnered Lives

In 2019, trend forecasters announced the emergence of the 'single positive' revolution, as a growing number of happy, fulfilled singles around the world view singledom as a conscious choice instead of an unfortunate holding period. A Future Laboratory trend report cited Euromonitor's prediction that by 2030, single-person households will be growing at a faster rate than any other household type around the world. 'For some, singledom is not a state that they long to be out of, but a lifestyle choice with benefits,' Future Laboratory's report said. 'Family and marriage are no longer the primary focal relationships for consumers.' Another trend report, from Wunderman Thompson Intelligence, called 'The Single Age', claimed: 'Single people are steadily becoming not outliers but a new norm, and they report finding great satisfaction in their decision.' Millennials, according to the report, are leading the movement.

It's also important to note 'single positives' aren't against being in a relationship—they simply won't settle for one that will bring unhappiness. It must expand their life, not reduce it. They do not need another half, they are whole already. Anything else is an addition, so the bar is set higher than it once was. The Future Laboratory is calling this shift the 'uncoupling of society', as we make a gradual move away from coupledom being seen as the cultural norm. And with this, singledom will be a choice, not a state of waiting.

In the 2019 December issue of British *Vogue*, actress Emma Watson graced the cover and spoke about broaching her thirtieth birthday the following April. She admitted she'd had a tough year, mainly because she had envisioned what her life would look like at thirty. At twenty-nine, she began feeling anxious and she soon realised it was because there was 'this bloody influx of subliminal messaging around'. It told her that if she did not have a husband, baby, home, and stable career by thirty, she was somehow a failure. 'There's just this incredible amount of anxiety,' she told the magazine. 'It took me a long time, but I'm very happy [being single]. I call it being self-partnered.'

Millennials are three times less likely than their grand-parents to marry, with marriage at an all-time low across the globe. In the United States, only 29 per cent of people aged between eighteen and thirty-four were married in 2018, compared to 59 per cent in 1978. Overall, only half of adults in the U.S. are married, and 51 per cent—more than half—of Americans aged between eighteen and thirty-four don't have a steady romantic partner. A 2014 Pew Research Center report predicted that by the time today's young men and women are fifty, at least one in four of us will have been single our entire lives. As marriage rates continue to decline and singledom continues to rise, it is leaving room for a huge percentage of people to not only live self-partnered lives, but thrive in them.

A New Emergence into Adulthood

I do not tell you these stories to persuade you into eternal singledom. I tell you these stories to remind you of the reality in which we live. A reality in which we don't have to settle, in which a true partnership is no longer a compulsory destination in our life, but merely a route we may choose to take if the fork appears in the road for us. It is a choice, not an obligation. Our life does not depend on it, is no longer defined by it, and continues to evolve without it. We are not a work in progress until we choose this route.

And if this is our new reality, if this is the current world women are able to live in because of the battles won by the women before them, our emergence into adulthood should no longer be defined by the drop of a knee, the appearance of a ring, a stroll down the aisle, or the arrival of a teammate. It should be defined by something far more intrinsic: our shift from dependence to independence. I am not talking about political, economic and civic independence, when we turn eighteen or twenty-one or whatever age the country we are living in deems as legal adulthood. I am talking about emotional independence. Where we not only know what it means to be ourselves, but respect the person who appears before us in the mirror each morning.

It should be defined by the love that arrives purely—and only—in ourselves.

This arrival point differs for each one of us, and what arrives is self-worth. You are, finally, enough. You are enough when you succeed. You are enough when you fail. You are enough when you walk out of your apartment feeling good as hell. You are enough when he doesn't call. You are, in every instance, enough.

See, self-worth is different to self-esteem, which tends to ebb and flow with the situations playing out before our lives. Self-worth is our rudder. Firmly attached, guiding us through the wins and losses of daily existence, getting us back on track a little faster each time. Creating a consistent undercurrent of resilience in our lives. So, when this self-worth arrives, when we depart dependence and reach emotional independence, that is something to celebrate.

And that is why everybody loves Lizzo. Her music is a celebration of the love that has arrived purely—and only—in herself, and she has become the soundtrack of this new emergence into adulthood.

A Life of One's Own

When this emergence into adulthood occurs, when this moment, for you, finally arrives, it is important to celebrate. Maybe you don't need to perform in front of a giant inflatable arse at the VMAs, but you do need to give this new chapter the recognition it deserves, whether it is a public act or a private one.

Maybe it's cracking open a bottle of Dom Pérignon with your closest girlfriends, maybe it's throwing a party to rival some of those weddings you've attended, or maybe it's moving into a new apartment and buying furniture you want to cohabitate with for the rest of your life. I personally love the last. Out with the Ikea, in with the Eames. Adulthood is here. Get the puppy if you were waiting for it too. You are no longer in a state of waiting. Your new chapter is here, you have made a choice. You have arrived. Anything else arriving beyond this point merely expands your life, but it does not define it. *You* do. And this, my friend, is an honour. Because we can experience something our mothers rarely could.

Earlier this month, the month I will have filed this book, it was my mother's fifty-seventh birthday. Someone once told me it is important to remember that your parents lived lives before you, and live lives beyond you, so you should ask them questions. These questions mean something to them, but also to you, because you usually learn things you never would have. So, I have started to ask my mother and father questions.

On my mother's fifty-seventh birthday I asked her whether she missed being young, which she did, whether she liked being 'old', which she did, and what her favourite years have been. The final question was a loaded one, because I assumed those years would be current ones. They were not. She missed her late twenties, when she had a job, an independent life, when she was with my father. She was not married for a lot of it, but in the later years she was. The defining factor of these years, though, was not marriage. It wasn't even a partner. It was that she didn't yet have children. She went to dinner parties, and had more fun after them, she went on weekenders and long holidays. The boundaries were fairly limitless and her life, full and fun. When we arrived, the good years departed.

What upset me about this was not that I amounted to the departure of her good years, but that her good years departed before she reached her early thirties, the decade I cannot wait to greet. The decade I have heard so much about, when women, I am told, experience self-actualisation and emotional fulfillment, and through this, gain an ease in themselves. Where they care less, and do more. I was upset my mother did not experience these years without being a mother to one, and soon two, and later, three children.

In my mother's era, and indeed her mother's, womanhood was defined by motherhood alongside the title of 'wife'. And as we now exist in an era that values emotional fulfillment above all else, it is no longer compulsory to become a mother or a wife. Despite the outdated cultural narrative that sometimes swirls around you. Despite the aunties who ask if you've had any 'joy' on the dating front, and the Pity Face you're on the receiving end of at weddings, and the nudge you get from Uncle John when the bouquet is about to be thrown or 'Single Ladies' comes on. Despite the questions and assumptions and looks that try to push you down this path because it is 'normal' for a woman to do, when it is not.

Merriam-Webster defines 'womanhood' as 'the distinguishing character or qualities of a woman or of womankind', and right now, the only common thread I see through the women I know is that they are walking their own paths and living an incredibly diverse range of lives.

There is Patti, the best young mother and the best creative director I know, spending her days making things as gorgeous as her children. There are Jessica and Honey, one a journalist, the other a PR associate, living together in New York. Neither has a partner right now but both lead incredible lives I cannot look at too often or I will jump on a plane. There is Laura, running her own business in Sydney. Katia, writing and living with her boyfriend overseas. There is Nat, who has just acquired her first apartment solo, fortunately in the street behind me. There is Souad, who has just moved with her boyfriend to Singapore. There are Cara and Julia, who are both recently engaged and Lara, a beauty marketing executive who moved from London to Sydney to find a new place to call home and a great love. There is Edwina, who has a life so full a man good enough to fill it hasn't yet arrived. There is Holly, who has come full circle to fall in love, again, with her high-school sweetheart in London. There is Angie, who has left me for New York to head up a publishing company and find an apartment of her own, one she has been waiting her entire life for. There is Jess, a model and writer who splits her time between Papua New Guinea, Australia and LA. There is Lucie, who has just become a barrister.

And then there are three incredible women in their fifties and sixties, whom I have grown to know over the past decade. Jen renovates houses better than anyone I know and tells compelling story after compelling story from her time in the corporate world. Helen has the respect and adoration of an entire industry, and a new business that is growing wings. Deb is one of the most creatively fulfilled people I have crossed paths with. Two are divorced, one has since remarried, and the other has never married and seems pretty pleased with this decision. But that is not how I like to define them. They sit at the forefront of my mind, right now, because of who they are and what they know and what I, as a result of listening to them, have learned. They are, above all else, fascinating company.

In fact, all of these women I mention are defined by who they are and what they do, more than their relationship status. Some may spend the majority of their lives single. Some may marry, some may have children and some won't. Some may investigate becoming mothers, alone, with more help from technology than a reliable man. And that is the era of womanhood we now live in.

Motherhood and wifehood once defined womanhood. But as women live lives with children and without them, with partners and alone, the only consistent undercurrent of women's lives is not one that involves the accessory of a husband or a child. It involves the presence of emotional fulfillment and emotional independence, which I guess defines the new era of womanhood entirely. An era in which we give back to ourselves.

I have been encouraging you to find a love that allows you to be limited only by yourself. But I don't want you, and the women you know, to be limited by yourselves either. I want the love that arrives purely—and only—within yourselves to be whole and strong and free. As Lizzo said in her VMA performance: 'It's so hard to love yourself in a world that doesn't love you back . . . So, I just want to take this opportunity right now to just feel good as hell. Because you deserve to feel good as hell. We deserve to feel good as hell.'

I want this love to be the destination you hope to reach more than anything else. I want this to be where you position your focus, where you put in the work, feeling good as hell as much as you possibly can along the way. The rest is merely an addition. An addition of course worth celebrating. But if *the rest* doesn't arrive for you, you are not losing out. You are gaining something many women before you— possibly your mother, and her mother—have not had the opportunity to acquire.

When you look back, you will see this book is structured around finding self-worth and emotional independence as much as it is a book about finding love. It is about rising above the patriarchal socialisation that encourages women to view ourselves in relation to man and prevents us, instead, from finding fulfillment in ourselves; and respecting ourselves enough to find and build and demand a love that allows us to reach our full potential. This book helps you find the power in being yourself, to have the confidence to go after what you want, take charge of your desires, maintain financial independence, find worth irrespective of beauty, trust the process because you know your worth, find happiness outside of relationships, maintain your drive within them because you know it is as important as his. And maybe most importantly, this book helps you own your ambition and your desires and your success in front of men, whether on a first date or three years in. Because this ambition, these desires, these successes fulfil you and make you who you are. They allow you to maintain emotional independence and remain in the beautiful chapter of adulthood you have spent all the chapters before it striving to reach. Regardless of whether you are in a relationship or not.

Over the process of reading this book, I hope you have grown to know yourself a little better and trust yourself a little more, to in turn own who you are and what you want. When you have a tight hold of these two things, it is not only easier to stumble upon the right man and the right relationship—it is easier to stumble upon self-worth and emerge into adulthood with your Dom Pérignon or new Eames chair or Bernese Mountain Dog. And this point of your life is something to aspire to as much as the wedding and the teammate.

If you do the work, if you realign your mindset toward finding the love you experience purely—and only—in yourself, you will reach a destination of liberation. A liberated love that says, as Maya Angelou did, 'I love you if you're in China. I love you if you're across town. I love you if you're in Harlem. I love you . . . Go.' A love that believes you are not just equal, you are enough. And with the arrival of this liberated love, you will not be living a life limited, only by yourself. You will be living a limitless one.

You will, in fact, be free.

Acknowledgements

This book was influenced by a certain chapter in my life. To all my girlfriends who were a part of that chapter, thank you. Lucie, Katia, Laura, Holly, Edwina and Honey, there are countless stories I didn't include, but your collective brilliance was the inspiration behind the premise. To all the fuckboys who were also a part of this chapter, thank you. I couldn't have written it without you.

To my former colleagues at *The Australian Women's Weekly*, I don't think you have any idea how much influence you had on me, but you taught me how to write a story and inspired me to keep going in a climate that does not reward the writer like it once did. Helen, I am forever indebted to you for taking a chance on me; for opening the door, and giving me the degree I actually needed.

Jane, thank you for taking notice of my work, and loving it enough to give me the chance to turn it into a book. Julie and Claire, thank you for pushing me even when I may not have wanted it. As you promised, this book is all the better for it and that is really all down to you. It has been an honour to be edited by you both and I feel like a different writer than the one who handed in the first draft. And to Lisa and the rest of the team at Murdoch Books: I may not see your faces regularly, but know the dedication and care you have all put into this book. It is an honour to be published by you and to have so many brilliant minds improving my work.

To my former colleagues at *Future Women*, thank you for putting up with me while I was writing every weekend. Kate, for being my constant confidante and counsellor and looking at one hundred thousand covers with me. You don't know how much of a rock you have been in my life, and I know you are that calming force for many. Patti, for being my circle. I hope the Patti Tears have already arrived, but if they haven't, thank you for putting my work into your brain, and delivering such a beautiful cover. I wouldn't have wanted it to be in anyone else's brain but yours. I am probably reading *Square* right now, and while that means I am in mid-existential crisis, it also means you're calming me down again. Jam, words cannot describe how much you have done for me. Thank you for guiding me through this process; from the negotiation, to filing the first draft, to the edits, to talking me off the ledge when *the doubt* arrived, and it arrived hard. You backed me in and helped me navigate this world from my first phone call. It is an honour to call you my friend.

To my other girlfriends—Souad, Lara, Cara, Jess, Jules— thank you for enduring countless conversations about this book over coffee and wine and also for understanding when I go MIA into a writing hole. I have many wines to catch up on. Beautiful Ang and Jess Vander Slay (Dean started calling you this, it stuck), I am so glad our work crossed paths, and even if we go months without a phone call, it is always the same. Thank you for being my creative buddies. To my girlfriends from school, Lara, Demi, Elle, and Anna, I know I have not been around much lately and I didn't tell you why until this book was done but our friendships are a bit like family. Time may get away from us, but it doesn't change much. It has been amazing to watch your lives expand, and see your partnerships (and families) grow.

To Porch and Parlour, thank you for the superior coffee and often being the only social interaction I have in a weekend. To Childish Gambino, Chance The Rapper, Kanye West, Jay Z, André 3000, Saint Jhn, and Lizzo, thank you for keeping me company while I write. The Deep Focus playlist also deserves a mention. Also, Dave Chapelle, John Mulaney, Michael Che, Pete Davidson, and Seth Meyers—thank you for keeping me entertained while I was reclusive. For the YouTube spirals, and the Netflix specials, and genuinely feeling like my friends even though you have no idea who I am.

Finally, thank you to my family. To both of my grandparents, you've shown me the value of a true and lasting partnership. Grandma and Grandpa, your mailbag book is always sitting underneath my coffee table and your mutual love of writing and reading has led me here. Grandma and Poppy, your relationship is beyond its time and the matriarch/Mayor of Port Elliot has a lot to answer for when it comes to my attitude. I know you will all probably disagree with half of this book and don't quite see yourselves as feminists yet, but you are. To Esther and Hannah, I won the sibling lottery. Thank you for being sisters I can always call on; for giving me shit constantly but having my back when necessary. As Zoe Saldana said on *The Conversation*, we have each other and that is all we ever need. To my parents, I owe you the world. Thank you for giving up so much to give me an education. You have always pushed me to do my best, but loved me unconditionally. I have paid witness to a solid life partnership, and one so many people—including your daughters—admire.

Dean, thank you for making me braver, for being my greatest adviser, best friend, editor, and most importantly, teammate. Even when you have to impale your leg onto a rock to get some attention. I was planning on thanking you further but you're hungry, so now we are going to buy food.

Further Reading and References

Chapter 1: The Rise of RBG and R-E-S-P-E-C-T

Allgeier, Elizabeth Rice and Wiederman, Michael W., 'Love and Mate Selection in the 1990s', *Free Inquiry* 11, no. 3, 1991, pp 25-27.

Coontz, Stephanie, *Marriage, a History: How Love Conquered Marriage*, Penguin, New York, 2006.

Crabb, Annabel, *The Wife Drought*, Ebury Press, Sydney, 2014.

Ely, Robin J., Stone, Pamela and Ammerman, Colleen, 'Rethink What You "Know" About High-Achieving Women', *Harvard Business Review*, December 2014.

Hewitt, Belinda, Western, Mark and Baxter, Janeen, *Marriage and Money: The Impact of Marriage on Men's and Women's Earnings*, 2002.

Kephart, William M., 'Some Correlates of Romantic Love', *Journal of Marriage and the Family* 29, no. 3, 1967, pp 470–74.

RBG, film produced by CNN Films, distributed by Magnolia Pictures, New York City, 2018.

West, Lindy. 'Her Loss', *New York Times*, 9 November 2016.

Chapter 2: Removing the Roadblocks

Bavel, Jan Van, Schwartz, Christine R and Esteve, Albert, 'The Reversal of the Gender Gap in Education and its Consequences for Family Life', *Annual Review of Sociology*, pp 341–360; VI 44; IP 1, 2018, doi: 10.1146/annurev-soc-073117-041215.

Bursztyn, Leonardo, Fujiwara, Thomas and Pallais, Amanda, '"Acting Wife": Marriage Market Incentives and Labor Market Investments', *American Economic Review*, 107 (11), pp 3288-3319, 2017, doi:10.1257/aer.20170029.

Fisman, Raymond, Iyengar, Sheena S., Kamenica, Emir and Simonson, Itamar, 'Gender Differences in Mate Selection: Evidence from a Speed Dating Experiment', *The Quarterly Journal of Economics* 121, no. 2, 2006, pp 673–97, www.jstor.org/stable/25098803.

Gerson, Kathleen, 'Moral Dilemmas, Moral Strategies, and the Transformation of Gender: Lessons from Two Generations of Work and Family Change', *Gender and Society*, 16(1), 2002, pp 8–28. www.jstor.org/stable/3081874.

Gerson, Kathleen, 'What Do Women and Men Want?', *The American Prospect*, 20 February 2007.

Greitemeyer, Tobias, 'What Do Men and Women Want in a Partner? Are Educated Partners Always More Desirable?', *Journal of Experimental Social Psychology*, 43, 2007, pp 180–194. 10.1016/j.jesp.2006.02.006.

Marriage Story, film produced by Heyday Films, Los Angeles and New York City, distributed by Netflix, 2019.

Qian, Yue, 'Gender Asymmetry in Educational and Income Assortative Marriage', *Journal of Marriage and Family*, Fam Relat, 79, 2017, pp 318–36, doi:10.1111/jomf.12372.

Ratliff, Kate A. and Oishi, Shigehiro, 'Gender differences in implicit self-esteem following a romantic partner's success or failure', *Journal of Personality and Social Psychology*, 105(4), 2013, pp 688–702, https://doi.org/10.1037/a0033769.

Schwartz, Christine R. and Gonalons-Pons, Pilar, 'Trends in Relative Earnings and Marital Dissolution: Are Wives Who Outearn Their Husbands Still More Likely to Divorce?', *The Russell Sage Foundation Journal of the Social Sciences: RSF*, 2(4), 2016, pp 218–236, https://doi.org/10.7758/rsf.2016.2.4.08.

Schwartz, Christine R. and Han, Hongyun, 'The Reversal of the Gender Gap in Education and Trends in Marital Dissolution', *American Sociological Review*, 79(4), 2014, pp 605–629, https://doi.org/10.1177/0003122414539682.

Smith, Zadie, *Feel Free*, Hamish Hamilton, London, 2018.

Syrda, Joanna, 'Spousal Relative Income and Male Psychological Distress', *Personality and Social Psychology Bulletin*, 2019, https://doi.org/10.1177/0146167219883611.

Zentner, Marcel, 'This is what dating could look like 100 years in the future', *Quartz*, 27 December 2017.

Zentner, Marcel and Eagly, Alice H., 'A Sociocultural Framework for Understanding Partner Preferences of Women and Men: Integration of Concepts and Evidence', *European Review of Social Psychology*, 26:1, 2015, pp 328–373, doi:10.1080/10463283.2015.1111599.

Chapter 3: You Can Make the First Move, but Not Three

Eastwick, Paul W., Eagly, Alice H., Glick, Peter, et al, 'Is Traditional Gender Ideology Associated with Sex-Typed Mate Preferences? A Test in Nine Nations', *Sex Roles*, 54, 2006, pp 603–14, https://doi.org/10.1007/s11199-006-9027-x.

Ledgerwood, Angela, 'Caitlin Moran: My Favourite Things', *Future Women*, 10 July 2018.

MacGregor, Jennifer and Cavallo, Justin, 'Breaking the Rules: Personal Control Increases Women's Direct Relationship Initiation', *Journal of Social and Personal Relationships*, 28(6), 2011, pp 848–67, 10.1177/0265407510397986.

O'Connor, Clare, 'Billion-Dollar Bumble: How Whitney Wolfe Herd Built America's Fastest-Growing Dating App', *Forbes Magazine*, 12 December 2017.

Zentner, Marcel, 'This is What Dating Could Look Like 100 Years in the Future', *Quartz*, 27 December 2017.

Zentner, Marcel and Eagly, Alice H., 'A Sociocultural Framework for Understanding Partner Preferences of Women and Men: Integration of Concepts and Evidence', *European Review of Social Psychology*, 26:1, 2015, pp 328–373, doi:10.1080/10463283.2015.1111599.

Chapter 4: Get the Bill

Newman, Andrew Adam, 'Acquisitive Craigslist Post Reddens Faces All Around', *New York Times*, 8 October 2007.

Chapter 5: You're Too Cool

Flynn, Gillian, *Gone Girl*, Crown, New York, 2012.

My Next Guest Needs No Introduction with David Letterman, Season 2, Episode 1, produced and distributed by Netflix, Los Gatos, California, 2019.

Ruiz, Don Miguel, *The Four Agreements: A Practical Guide To Personal Freedom*, Amber-Allen Publishing, San Rafael, California, Inc., 1997.

Chapter 6: Know What You Want, and Talk About It

Bursztyn, Leonardo, Fujiwara, Thomas and Pallais, Amanda, '"Acting Wife": Marriage Market Incentives and Labor Market Investments', *American Economic Review*, 107, 11, 2017, pp 3288–3319, 10.1257/aer.20170029, http://www.aeaweb.org/articles?id=10.1257/aer.20170029

Obama, Michelle, *Becoming*, Crown, New York, 2018.

Sandberg, Sheryl, *Lean In: Women, Work, and the Will to Lead*, Knopf, New York, 2013.

Walker, Kristi, Bialik, Kristen and van Kessel, Patrick, 'Strong Men, Caring Women', Pew Research Center, 24 July 2018.

Chapter 7: Put the U Back in Beauty

Berger, John, *Ways Of Seeing*, BBC/Penguin, London, 1972.

Tolentino, Jia, *Trick Mirror: Reflections on Self-Delusion*, Random House, New York, 2019.

Widdows, Heather, *Perfect Me*, Princeton University Press, New Jersey, 2018.

Wolf, Naomi, *The Beauty Myth*, Chatto & Windus, London, 1990.

Chapter 8: Your Checklist Isn't Your Checklist

Eastwick, Paul W., Eagly, Alice H., Glick, Peter, et al, 'Is Traditional Gender Ideology Associated with Sex-Typed Mate Preferences? A Test in Nine Nations', *Sex Roles*, 54, 2006, pp 603–14, https://doi.org/10.1007/s11199-006-9027-x.

Fisman, Raymond, Iyengar, Sheena S., Kamenica, Emir and Simonson, Itamar. 'Gender Differences in Mate Selection: Evidence from a Speed Dating Experiment',

The Quarterly Journal of Economics 121, no. 2, 2006, pp 673–97, www.jstor.org/stable/25098803.

Gladwell, Malcolm, *Blink: The Power of Thinking without Thinking*, Little, Brown and Company, New York, 2005.

Zentner, Marcel, 'This is What Dating Could Look Like 100 Years in the Future', *Quartz*, 27 December 2017.

Zentner, Marcel and Eagly, Alice H., 'A Sociocultural Framework for Understanding Partner Preferences of Women and Men: Integration of Concepts and Evidence', *European Review of Social Psychology*, 26:1, 2015, pp 328–73, doi:10.1080/10463283.2015.1111599.

Chapter 9: Stop Looking for Him Instead of Yourself

Bennett, Jessica, 'It's a New Morning for Jennifer Aniston', *New York Times*, 10 September 2019.

Didion, Joan, 'Self-respect: Its Source, its Power', *Vogue* magazine, 1961.

Havrilesky, Heather, *How to Be a Person in the World: Ask Polly's Guide Through the Paradoxes of Modern Life*, Anchor, New York, 2016.

Lammer, Aaron, Linsky, Max and Ratliff, Evan, *Longform* podcast, 'Episode 182: Heather Havrilesky', 2 March 2016.

Winfrey, Oprah, *What I Know For Sure*, Flatiron Books, New York, 2014.

Chapter 10: He's Just Not That Into You, or It's Not About You

Bolick, Kate, 'All the Single Ladies', *The Atlantic* magazine, November 2011.

Bolick, Kate, *Spinster*, Broadway Books, New York, 2016.

Guttentag, Marcia and Secord, Paul F., *Too Many Women? The Sex Ratio Question*, SAGE Publications, Inc., Beverley Hills, 1983.

South, Scott J., and Trent, Katherine, 'Sex Ratios and Women's Choices: A Cross-National Analysis', *American Journal of Sociology*, Vol. 93, No. 5, 1988, pp. 1096–1115.

Teirney, Raewyn Dr., https://www.ivf.com.au/specialists/ivf-doctors-australia/dr-raewyn-teirney.

Chapter 11: Don't Let Aunty Carol and the Pity Face Get to You

DePaulo, Bella, 'What No One Ever Told You About People Who are Single', TED lecture, March 2017.

Dominus, Susan, 'Gloria Steinem: First Feminist', *New York* magazine, 6 April 1998.

Kramer, Jane, 'Road Warrior', *New York* magazine, 19 October 2015.

Watts, Alan, *The Wisdom of Insecurity*, Pantheon, New York, 1951.

Chapter 12: Have Your Own Shit, and Keep Doing It

Didion, Joan, *Slouching Towards Bethlehem*, Farrar, Straus and Giroux, New York, 1968.

Winfrey, Oprah, *Oprah's SuperSoul Conversations*. 'Oprah and Michelle Obama: Your Life in Focus', 12 February 2020.

Chapter 13: Diversify Your Love

Cheung, Elaine O., Gardner, Wendi L. and Anderson, Jason F., 'Emotionships: Examining People's Emotion-Regulation Relationships and Their Consequences for Well-Being', *Social Psychological and Personality Science*, Vol. 6, No. 4, 2015 pp 407–14.

Dunbar, Robin, *How Many Friends Does One Person Need? Dunbar's Number and Other Evolutionary Quirks*, Harvard University Press, Cambridge, Massachusetts, 2010.

Leaver, Kate, *The Friendship Cure*, HarperCollins Publishers, Sydney, 2018.

Perel, Esther, 'The Secret to Desire in a Long-Term Relationship', TED lecture, February 2013.

Perhach, Paulette, 'A Story of a Fuck Off Fund', *The Billfold*, 20 January 2016.

Chapter 14: New Game, New Wins

Baxter, Jennifer, 'Fathers and Work: A Statistical Overview', *Australian Institute of Family Studies*, May 2019.

Carlson, Dan L., Miller, Amanda J. and Sassler, Sharon, 'Stalled for Whom? Change in the Division of Particular Housework Tasks and Their Consequences for Middle- to Low-Income Couples', *Socius*, 2018, https://doi.org/10.1177/2378023118765867.

Crabb, Annabel, 'Men at Work', *Quarterly Essay*, Issue 75, September 2019.

Croft, Alyssa, Schmader, Toni, Block, Katharina and Baron, Andrew Scott, 'The Second Shift Reflected in the Second Generation: Do Parents' Gender Roles at Home Predict Children's Aspirations?', *Psychological Science*, 25(7), 2014, pp 1418–28. https://doi.org/10.1177/0956797614533968.

Garcia, Michael A. and Umberson, Debra, 'Marital Strain and Psychological Distress in Same-Sex and Different-Sex Couples', *Journal of Marriage and Family*, Fam Relat, 81(5), 2019, pp 1253–68, doi:10.1111/jomf.12582.

Gottman, John, Levenson, Robert, Swanson, Catherine, Swanson, Kristin, Tyson, Rebecca and Yoshimoto, Dan, 'Observing Gay, Lesbian and Heterosexual Couples' Relationships: Mathematical Modeling of Conflict Interaction', *Journal of Homosexuality*, 45(i), 2003, pp 65–91, 10.1300/J082v45n01_04.

McGinn, Kathleen L., Ruiz Castro, Mayra and Lingo, Elizabeth L., 'Learning from Mum: Cross-National Evidence Linking Maternal Employment and Adult Children's Outcomes', *Work, Employment and Society*, 33(3), 2019, pp 374–400, https://doi.org/10.1177/0950017018760167.

Rudman, Laurie A. and Phelan, Julie E., 'The Interpersonal Power of Feminism: Is Feminism Good for Romantic Relationships?', *Sex Roles*, 57(ii), 2007, pp 787–99, 10.1007/s11199-007-9319-9.

Tolentino, Jia, 'Please, My Wife, She's Very Online', *The New Yorker*, 5 June 2019.

Yavorsky, Jill E., Kamp Dush, Claire M. and Schoppe-Sullivan, Sarah J., 'The Production of Inequality: The Gender Division of Labor Across the Transition to Parenthood', *Journal of Marriage and Family*, 77 (3), 2015, pp 662–679, doi:10.1111/jomf.12189.

Chapter 15: Plan S(ingle)

Davis, Allison P., 'It's Just a Matter of Time Till Everybody Loves Lizzo', *The Cut*, 3 February 2019.

Houghton, Livvy and Walker, Daniela, 'Uncoupled Living', *LS:N Global*, a division of *The Future Laboratory*, 14 March 2019.

Lees, Paris. 'Emma Watson on Being Happily "Self-Partnered" at 30', British *Vogue*, December 2019.

Wang, Wendy and Parker, Kim, 'Record Share of Americans Have Never Married', Pew Research Center, 24 September 2014.

Wunderman Thompson Intelligence (formerly) The Innovation Group, 'New Trend Report: The Single Age', *Wunderman Thompson*, 26 June 2019.

Index